UNDERSTANDING
TEENAGERS

UNDERSTANDING TEENAGERS

Pete Gilbert

Crossway Books
Nottingham

This book is dedicated to our daughter Frederica Clare,
a gift from God and a teenager of the future.

© Pete Gilbert 1993

First Edition 1993

ISBN 1 85684 030 1

The Scripture used in this work, unless indicated
otherwise, is taken from the New International Version of
the Bible, © 1978 by the New York International Bible
Society.

Typeset by Avocet Typesetters, Bicester, Oxon
Printed in Great Britain for Crossway Books by
Cox & Wyman Ltd, Reading, Berkshire

CONTENTS

PREFACE

Before you read any further in this book let me explain what it is not. This is not a book about parenting. As I began work on this book my wife was expecting our first child, which meant that I was not yet myself a parent and therefore had no experience or qualifications for telling others how best to parent their adolescent children. As I complete the book my daughter is now a year old. Therefore my experience of parenting adolescents thus far has all been on the receiving end, and I continue to marvel at the care, love and patience shown by my own parents through my adolescent years. The faults of the author are mainly his own, and not the result of his parents!

Nor is this a book about 'How to be a successful youth minister', or 'How to plan a youth programme'. I have been involved in church youth work, discipling and evangelism for the last fifteen years and, making many mistakes, have learned a few lessons along the way. There are a number of helpful books on the market which can teach you how to be a successful youth worker/programmer. This book does not aim to be one of them.

I have written this book with the express intention of

aiming it at parents and youth leaders, but with the sole purpose of helping them better understand the ever-changing world of the adolescent. It is my belief that while all good parenting and youth programmes do come out of the inspiration of the Holy Spirit, they also come out of the perspiration and preparation of the parent and the youth leader! This book is my own attempt at putting down a suitable framework of head-knowledge (Hos 4:6) and also heart-knowledge (Prov 29:18), which the Holy Spirit can then fill, or if he wishes, blow apart. It remains my conviction, and hopefully yours too, that only with such a framework of understanding and an overview of the world-picture of the adolescent, can the practical implications for your family and your church be understood and applied. It is to that end that I write this book.

I remain grateful to all the people who have influenced me in the writing of this book, not least my parents, the small youth group at a little Methodist Mission Hall in Cottingham, north Humberside (1975–1978), and the many churches I attempted to work with and serve in Waltham Forest, north-east London, during my time with British Youth for Christ (1978–1985). Of paramount importance to my thinking and experience have been my own church family – Revelation, A Church in the Community – where I have been exposed to and been a part of dynamic youth evangelism and discipleship, and Pioneer's TIE Teams (a training and development programme committed to seeing church leaders emerging from our youth). My thanks go to all these and many other individuals too numerous to mention. Many of the ideas and experiences we have shared together; the faults I claim as my own.

CHAPTER ONE

COMING TO TERMS

– SOME VITAL DEFINITIONS

Let it be noted at the outset that this book is about adolescen*ts*, not adolescen*ce*. I have two main reasons for making this distinction. Firstly, adolescence is a generic term and lends itself all too easily to theory and philosophy, whereas *Understanding Adolescents* is all about attempting to understand specific, unique individuals made in the image of God. Secondly, if we talk merely about adolescence, then we will be in grave danger of falling perpetually into the habit of stereotyping, where generalisations become the rule and where we lose sight of the fact that it is neither easy nor right to attempt to make people fit into simplistic and broad categories.

The chances are that as you read this book you will have in your mind a specific adolescent or group of adolescents, otherwise I doubt whether you would have bothered to pick the book up, or even considered purchasing it. I want to encourage you, as we begin together, to seek a frame-work of understanding adolescents, to keep those individuals in your heart and in your mind, for that will be a helpful and valid perspective to help keep our feet on the ground as well as our heads in the clouds! I would like us to be so heavenly-minded that we are of enormous earthly use when it comes to understanding adolescents.

A little history . . .

Of course, it is true to say that adolescence (and therefore adolescents!) has always been with us – there has always been a stage of 'growing up', but it is equally true to say that the various civilisations throughout world history have coped with adolescents in very different ways.

The psychological approach to understanding adolescents concerns mainly the *internalised* factors of change within the individual, and the pressures that he or she is experiencing, with the subsequent effects upon the individual's personality and, therefore, behaviour. The sociological approach to understanding adolescents favours more an examination of the *external* factors of environment – such as society, family, education – upon the lives of individual adolescents. Both are valid approaches and mainly products of the twentieth century. However, adolescence has been with us very much longer than that.

'When I look at the younger generation I despair for the future of civilisation!' This quotation could as readily come from a twentieth century sociologist as from the fourth century BC philosopher, Aristotle, who actually wrote it. 'Youth has no regard for old age, and the wisdom of the centuries is looked down upon both as stupidity and foolishness. The young men are indolent; the young women are indecent and indecorous in their speech, behaviour and dress.' And these twelfth century words of Peter the Hermit could as easily be transposed into the mouth of a hard-line twentieth century tele-evangelist.

Different ages have identified similar traits in the development of young people to adulthood, and though the solutions have differed across the ages, the causes have remained the same – the joys and the frustrations, the opportunities and the pitfalls of adolescence.

The rich tapestry of Jewish culture, from which our Bible came, had its own way of recognising and dealing with the issues of adolescence. Although it is true to say that the Jews had a specific ritual (bar mitzvah), by means of which they recognised the accession of the male child into recognised manhood at the age of thirteen, it would be simplistic to assume that in Jewish culture at the age of twelve a youth was viewed as a child, whilst at the age of thirteen the same youth was viewed as a man. The reason why the ceremony was reserved for males is both sociological and psychological. Sociological in that Jewish society was chauvinistic (Jesus eliminated many of those barriers when he came), and psychological in that for the female the onset of menstruation was both physiological and physically obvious and appropriate as an access point into adulthood, whereas for the male there was and remains no such obvious starting point. In any case, there was recognised in Jewish tradition (and also in the Bible) not a sudden bar mitzvah transition, but a progressive probationary period which is most accurately defined in biblical terms as 'youth', as opposed to 'childhood'.

Both the Old Testament Hebrew word for youth (*Naar*) and the New Testament Greek word (*Neanias*) denote the heroic and noble acts associated with youth, and are clearly seen as distinct from childhood. Thus, youth is defined in Leviticus 27 as being up to the age of twenty, not merely up to the age of thirteen (bar mitzvah). Judah's King Josiah was, at the age of sixteen (after eight years' rule), termed 'still young' (2 Chron 34:1–3). Similarly, there is a distinction drawn between children and young men in Jeremiah 6:11, and in Joel 2:28 there is a specific reference to the function of young men, as opposed to merely sons and daughters. The same distinctions are made in the New Testament in 1 John 2:12–14, where the categories are children, young men and fathers. And the category 'young men' makes an appearance in Titus 2:6.

Our conclusion is that in Jewish culture, notwithstanding

a helpful celebration of the onset of adulthood – we will look at why and how this is helpful in later chapters – there was none-the-less a recognised development period before full adulthood was recognised. This period, which we would term adolescence, seems to have run between the ages of thirteen to twenty.

Nor were the Jews alone in recognising this period. The Roman civilisation had its own version of adolescence, but they seem to have set the period between the ages of seventeen to twenty-eight. Their outward show or celebration, the Roman version of the Jewish bar mitzvah, was that the youth would cease to wear the Roman short tunic and would now be eligible to wear the Roman toga.

In the Middle Ages across much of Europe, the period of youth was recognised as running from seven years to the late twenties, although again, at a fairly crucial mid-point (age fourteen), a young male could go through a religious ceremony pledging himself to a knight, as a form of discipleship, and could therefore become a squire.

There are many other recorded civilisations, some current, which also exercise some ritual or initiation ceremony whereby the male youth is recognised as an adult and as such *begins* to take his place in adult society. For the female, such ceremonies or rites always revolve around the onset of menstruation, whilst for the male, the ceremonies range from the religious to the perhaps more atavistic hunting ceremonies, trials of strength, or rites of physical circumcision at or around puberty.

And more recently . . .

The advent of the industrial revolution in this country brought with it the terrible (and often realised) potential for the inhuman oppression of many young people. As our society struggled through a period of great upheaval and a shift in wealth, power, and workforce from the agricultural to the industrial, so also government gradually began to recognise the special needs of young people. And so in 1833 and 1847 the Factory Acts came into being, and to an extent protected the working rights of a special group of people, singled out by their age only – the thirteen- to eighteen-year-olds. In 1834 some of the severity of the harsh legal and penal system was lessened by the Youthful Offenders Act, which now distinguished between young and adult criminal offenders. It was also in the 1830s that education made a crucial distinction between primary and secondary phases, placing the watershed at the age of thirteen, an age later *sociologically* identified as the access point 'teenager'. A recognised group of people, with specific rights, was beginning to emerge in the time around and immediately after the industrial revolution, and this group was defined exclusively by its age. And so, by the 1850s specific pamphlets and then books (the precursors of the teenage comic and magazine) began to emerge aimed at that particular bracket of people.

And so on . . .

It has not been insignificant that in our own more recent society the emergence of the adolescent has gone alongside the development of the need to protect (the legal system), to punish (the judicial system), and to propagate wares (the marketing system). If in our recent history it was the industrial revolution which first identified the group which has now come to be known as adolescents, then in the twentieth century it has been a spin-off from that industrial revolution – marketing and consumerism – which has created a whole adolescent or youth culture, and coined the word 'teenager' to boot.

The word teenager – denoting one who is in his or her teens (thirteen–nineteen-year-olds) – was first coined in about 1942, during the Second World War, by market researchers looking to identify a category of young people at whom they could target their wares. From the forties to the fifties this category of youth was identified as a prime target, particularly in the areas of music and fashion, because they above other sections of the consumer market had the most uncommitted cash. Those who were younger did not have enough cash; those who were older had too many responsibilities and calls upon the cash that they did have. It was those in the middle, the adolescents, who were seen as the most lucrative fair game. And so industries of communication through magazines, comics, records, and later tapes, videos, TV, films, and so on, all zeroed in on a profitable market, which by the mid-1980s in this country was estimated at £2,000 million per annum.

For the adolescent the post-war, care-free fifties (with the advent of rock-'n'-roll) gave way to the heady hedonism of the sixties (with the advent of the Beatles), followed by the idyllic idealism of the seventies (hippies, flower-power, drugs, gurus and cults), and so into the disillusionment of the eighties (AIDS, riots and street violence, mass unemployment), and the restless searching of the nineties (and an increasing momentum of both evangelism *and* New Age philosophy).

Increasing awareness of the material states of our two-thirds world and the ravages our one third world have wreaked upon the global environment has forced its way into the adolescent consciousness. The cruel god of materialism has been revealed to have feet of clay, but historically the adolescent is still paying a heavy price from the legacy of materialism.

The emphasis which the post-war generations in this country have placed upon materialism (where 'what you own' and 'what you do' is 'what you are worth' as a person), has led to a continued emphasis on the economically viable nuclear family (Mum and Dad, plus two) and a clear demonstration that without God, ideals are not possible (with one in three of those marriages in the UK ending in divorce). Material gain, so important to our western culture, has meant that the nuclear family is one of the strongest components to financial security, as opposed to the extended family of many other cultures. One of the deficiencies of the nuclear family, however, is that it has denied many young people the opportunity of growing up around old people, and this in turn has tended to exacerbate the generation gap.

The generation gap can easily be over-emphasised, whereas it must be borne in mind that young people grow up developing by and large the same values and standards as those of their parents and adults around them. However, there is truth in the observation that we are not only developing a whole generation of young people with little or no experience of relating to the elderly, but often deny those same young people the vital role model of a father in the family home, as more and more nuclear families break down. We will look at the implications of this in more detail in Chapter 5.

Don't mention the war

At a time when many traditional taboos have fallen; when the war can be talked about with impunity as Germany reunifies; as sex occupies most of our tabloids and television programmes (though the more we talk about it, the more convinced I am that for many it remains a taboo subject); as world religions, cults and the occult play an ever more central part in world affairs; as politics become prime-time TV viewing; there yet remain two main taboos in our western society. The first is how much a person earns. The second is death.

Western society has successfully continued to successively anaesthetise the western mind and experience when it comes to the subject of death and dying. As people live longer, and the UK population grows older, so our geriatric wards fill up and our dying are ushered into sanitised hospices or clinicised sanitoriums. From death to probate can now be the work of a week. Chapels of Rest are largely things of the past, and the number of people, let alone young people, who have actually seen and/or touched a dead body seems to be ever decreasing. Could it be that this is partly because of western society's flirtation with the cult of youth versus death? I think so. Where once young people were simply smaller versions of their parents and the adults around them (the mediaeval idea of the homunculus?), it is now more demonstratively the other way round! Youth culture has become dominant beyond the extent of its years in many aspects of fashion, communication, and entertainment, whether it be from the nature of background music played in high street boutiques, that barbers are now hairdressers, or that yesterday's youth fashion labels are today's adult fashion labels. In many ways today's society (including the adults) has become retrogressive, looking back to some golden Utopian age, which never actually existed.

Hopefully, this brief overview of the history of adolescence, and why it is so deeply rooted in our modern society, has been of some help to you. It does however beg one major question.

What *is* an adolescent?

The Oxford English Dictionary defines an adolescent as 'a person growing up between childhood and manhood or womanhood'. The key factor to note here is that adolescents are between stages. They are on a journey through life. They may well be fully adult in the physical sense of that word; they may have already developed to the maximum of their mental capacity (though probably not to their academic capacity). But nonetheless there will be other areas in which the adolescent is not fully adult. In understanding the terms used throughout this book, and in order to help us understand the adolescent that we actually know, we must avoid the assumption that wherever a young person is not adult, he or she is automatically a child. There is an in-between stage. *This* is the stage of the adolescent.

You will have already noted that different societies and cultures at different times have placed the age range of the adolescent within different parameters. There is no one simple helpful criterion to use when defining the age range of adolescence; most sociologists and psychologists would agree that puberty may start (particularly in girls) well before the onset of adolescence proper. So we cannot use merely physical boundaries. Some young lads will begin puberty at eleven, others will not begin it until sixteen when the first group are nearing the end of puberty. We need a more holistic approach to determining the approximate age span which covers the state of adolescence. The reason for this is simple.

Areas of change

I want to suggest that there are five key areas of change within the life of your specific adolescent. I want to devote a subsequent chapter to each area, but for now let's list them.

Physical change
Emotional change
Mental change
Social change
Spiritual change

When God breaks into a person's life to bring salvation, it is to affect all five of these areas. That is because the New Testament Greek word for salvation (*soterio*) means wholeness, healing, salvation. God is not just interested in saving 'souls', but in redeeming whole people. This is true for any of us, but it is never more true than for the adolescent. The reason for this is evident: during adolescence, as at no other time, all of the five life areas are changing fundamentally *at the same time*. Never again does this happen with such dramatic effect. This is why our definition of adolescence must be holistic and not just dependent on *one* life area such as the physical.

Sociologists identify key times of stress in the life of the average individual: marriage, change of home, change of job, bereavement, retirement. If you are a parent or a youth leader you might want to add 'dealing with adolescents' to that list! However, even in these times of stress, it is true to say that the life areas do not change to the same degree, or with as little comparative experience, as at adolescence. The adolescent on his/her journey between childhood and adulthood, is in a state of flux in all five interrelated life areas. Imagine it as the huge gong at the beginning of a Rank Film! The gong represents the life of the adolescent. The stick which hits the gong is the onset of adolescence (which can often be the onslaught of puberty!). And the whole gong reverberates to produce the note. So too with the life of the adolescent; healthy maturity comes when all five interrelated areas of change are developing simultaneously. But, let the reader beware! The 'vibrations' through the life of the adolescent can be severe; 'discord' is not uncommon!

If we are to understand the world of the adolescent and the areas of change within him/her, then a closer look at each area will be necessary later. But let me start the next chapter by asking one further question.

CHAPTER TWO

WHY BOTHER?

– OUR MOTIVATIONS

There are five reasons why we need to bother about understanding adolescents. The first reason is to release compassion. It is a fact of life that that which we do not understand we tend to fear. There are many commands in the Bible not to be afraid (366 of them – which equates to one for each day of the year, including leap years!), and fear is fought with faith, hope, love, and with understanding.

The Bible teaches that we are to understand ourselves, others, the Enemy, and God. What we do not understand, we fear. What we fear, we tend to fight against. If we are to be clothed with compassion and sent out into a ravening world as sheep among wolves (Mt 10:16–32) then we must hold fast to the fact that people (yes, even your rebellious son/daughter, or that clique in the youth group that won't integrate, or that class of snarling fifth years!) are *not* the enemy (Eph 6:12), and that we see them not for their problems, but for their potential. Compassion will help us get rid of fear (as does God's compassion for us (1 Jn 4:18).

Nowhere is this compassion better demonstrated than in the life and teaching of Jesus Christ. He was the man who, leaving the multitude, crossed the lake in order to deal with one individual (Mk 5), and then taught about it in the form of a parable (Lk 15). He was the man who wept at the grave of his friend and went on to do something practical about it (Jn 11:35). This same man wept over the city of Jerusalem (Mt 23:37). And, it was he who, unlike other rabbis of his day, placed a high value on the worth of young people (Jn 6:9, Mt 18:1–6, 19:13–15) – we will see more of this and why in Chapter 3.

Such compassion cannot be whipped up, or artificially created. The word compassion comes from two Latin words, which together mean 'with pain', and pain and passion are closely linked in Scripture, almost as often as pain and adolescence! There are two practical ways that I know of to increase your compassion.

The first is the John 6 Multiplication Syndrome. Significantly, this demonstration of compassion by Jesus involves a young boy. The principle operates as follows: Jesus, having compassion on the crowds around him (unlike his disciples) takes the five loaves and two fishes – ie, the little which the boy had – and after thanking God for them and breaking them, miraculously causes multiplication to take place by means of which many individuals (a minimum of 5,000, since that number would not have included the women and children) are fed, with some food to spare. Now, when it comes to compassion, the principle is the same. You take the little you already have (you must have some or you wouldn't be trying to understand adolescents in the first place), and you give it to Jesus who will take it, give thanks for it and break it. A word of warning here: as Jesus breaks your compassion you may find that it breaks your heart and could be a painful experience as you begin to get *God's* perspective on youth. He will then give what little you had back to you and you will find that by supernatural multiplication your compassion is able to satisfy the individual demands of many. This is not a preacher's rhetoric, it actually works.

Secondly, there is a spiritual gift (charismata, or grace gift) of compassion, which is as available to you as are any of God's good gifts (Lk 11:13, Jas 1:17). The gift of compassion is no different – you have a gift when you ask for it in faith, receive it in faith, and then *use it*. So, God will multiply the compassion that you have, and he will also give to you a gift of compassion, if you ask for it and are prepared to use it.

Confidence

Understanding adolescents will also promote confidence in our approach to them. Ultimately, of course, it is the Holy Spirit who teaches and equips us and gives us the things which we need to say, under various testing circumstances (Mt 10:19–20). But the Holy Spirit has always looked for a framework to fill, a body to indwell, be it that first body of Jesus Christ on earth (Lk 3:21–22, 4:1) or the second body of Jesus Christ on earth, the Church (ie, you and me, Eph 5:18). 'Doing our homework' when it comes to understanding adolescents helps us to place our confidence not so much in the homework, as in the Holy Spirit's desire to fill that framework up. Information alone will lead us into frustration. But, information plus revelation will lead us to formation of our character, and implementation of God's will. Our faith needs to be linked to our works, so that we are both hearers and doers (Jas 1:22–25, 2:17–26).

Counsel

Understanding adolescents will enable our better counsel of them. When in the Old Testament David was assembling around him the strategic elements of the nation of Israel, preparatory to extending the kingdom (which latterly is the job of all disciples of Jesus), he drew around him men who understood 'the times' (1 Chron 12:32). If we are to dare to get involved in counselling the intricate lives of adolescents which are in the state of flux described earlier, then we must be men and women who understand the times in which they live and how they live in those times.

Communication

The greatest communicator in the Bible after Jesus was the Apostle Paul, who sets out in 1 Corinthians 9:16–27 his 'manifesto' on communication. Having experienced and understood the importance of the risen Christ, Paul seems to have been totally committed to incarnational communication. This is useful, because Paul's God was also committed to the same method! God has always been a God who incarnates his message. He created Adam and Eve as a living example of the love relationship which already existed between Father, Son and Holy Spirit. Adam and Eve were to become the first family on earth, because it is from God that all families take their name (as God himself – Father, Son and Holy Spirit – Eph 3:14–15). God's message was incarnated in the prophets, who not only had a message but were a message, as they lived out, sometimes through peculiar circumstances, the communication which God had given them. So we read of prophets marrying prostitutes, streaking through the streets, or lying for weeks on end facing piles of dung. Supremely, of course, God's incarnational communication has been in the person of his Son, Jesus Christ, who is the word made flesh (Jn 1:14, Heb 1:1–3).

Now Christians, as disciples of Jesus Christ, proudly bear his name – the name Christian was first used of followers of The Way at Antioch, and means literally 'little Christs'. Consequently, we are to incarnate our message just as Jesus did. Being good news as well as having good news will help us not only to live, but also to share our life with others. This most certainly includes adolescents, who use emulation as a primary means of learning. Young people, being quick to spot a fake and hating hypocrisy, will always respond more to who you are than what you say. Understanding adolescents, what influences them, who they are and what they think, is bound therefore to enhance our communication with them. And if we are being real and 'incarnating our communication', this can only be for the good. It is God's way of getting through to us, and can be our way of getting through to adolescents.

Conceptualisation

The fifth and final reason why we need to bother to understand adolescents is in order that our minds might be expanded. God is the God of all ages, not just the old, or the young. And one of the things which we can learn from youth is that we *do* still need to learn. In understanding adolescents we can learn again to learn, and as we realise the process which is involved in extending compassion, confidence, counsel and good communication towards adolescents, we will find it easier to reproduce ourselves in the lives of others.

Being a good parent or a good youth leader involves principles of Christian discipleship. Christian discipleship is about apprenticing, development and reproduction. Unless you and I conceptualise, come to understand what we are learning and why, we will never be able to develop others to their potential in Christ, nor be able to reproduce ourselves effectively in character, heart and ethos. It is biblical to do so (Col 1:9, 2:2, 1 Cor 14:20), but to do it effectively and biblically, we must learn to understand the adolescent, and we must learn to understand ourselves.

Do it yourself checklist

I leave this second chapter with three specific questions which I encourage you to answer.

1.   With a specific adolescent in mind, what do you like about that individual?

2.   What do you not like about that particular individual?

3.   What do you not understand about that particular individual?

I have tried this exercise many times in many different forums, both Christian and non-Christian, and the answers usually run to form. Answers to question one usually include: enthusiasm, honesty, loyalty, energy and idealism. Paradoxically, question two often elicits an opposite list encompassing: cliquiness, apathy, fickleness, rebellion, mood swings, insecurity, arrogance and selfishness. In the rest of the book we will see more clearly what the pluses and minuses of being an adolescent are. And why.

But first, a final word of warning. I have often found that the answers to question three can be the same as the answers to question two. If this was the case for you, can I suggest that in fact it is *you* who have the problem, not the adolescent? Remember that we tend to automatically dislike that which we cannot understand, for by such things we feel threatened. In understanding adolescents, we may not come to like everything about them, but we can at least see where they are coming from, and more helpfully point the way forward to where, by the love of God, they might arrive.

CHAPTER THREE

AND WHO IS MY NEIGHBOUR?

– OUR ATTITUDES

The Parable of the Good Samaritan

On one occasion an expert in the law stood up to test Jesus.
'Teacher,' he asked, 'what must I do to inherit eternal life?'
'What is written in the Law?' he replied. 'How do you read it?'
He answered: ' ''Love the Lord your God with all your heart
and with all your soul and with all your strength and with all
your mind'', and, ''Love your neighbour as yourself.'' '
'You have answered correctly,' Jesus replied. 'Do this and
you will live.'
But he wanted to justify himself, so he asked Jesus, 'And who
is my neighbour?'
In reply Jesus said: 'A man was going down from Jerusalem
to Jericho, when he fell into the hands of robbers. They stripped
him of his clothes, beat him and went away, leaving him half
dead. A priest happened to be going down the same road, and
when he saw the man, he passed by on the other side. So too,
a Levite, when he came to the place and saw him, passed by
on the other side. But a Samaritan, as he travelled, came where
the man was; and when he saw him, he took pity on him. He
went to him and bandaged his wounds, pouring on oil and
wine. Then he put the man on his own donkey, took him to

an inn and took care of him. The next day he took out two silver coins and gave them to the innkeeper. 'Look after him,' he said, 'and when I return, I will reimburse you for any expense you may have.'

'Which of these three do you think was a neighbour to the man who fell into the hands of robbers?'

The expert in the law replied, 'The one who had mercy on him.'

Jesus told him, 'Go and do likewise' (Lk 10:25–37).

The parable which you have just read is probably very familiar to you. The problem is, we can become too familiar with stories in the Bible and miss the points that they were originally intended to make. There is a great danger when it comes to dealing with parables in Scripture in that it is possible to go beyond the main points which the parable is making and to spiritualise small details which were never intended to carry particular meaning. Most of the parables that Jesus told were designed to:

a) Hide truth from those who would ridicule it, and

b) Make one or, at most, a very few points for those listeners who would let the parable challenge their lifestyle.

This particular parable is no different and I don't want to violate the text out of context, which would then simply make it a pretext for illustrating my argument! Also, I am indebted to Trevor Partridge of Crusade for World Revival for some of the ideas which I want to develop here.

Essentially then, the parable is the story of a traveller. We have already seen from Chapter 1 that a definition of an adolescent is one who is in turn a traveller on a journey. The adolescent's journey is between childhood and adulthood. Moreover, for reasons which we will explore later in the book in more detail, our adolescent on his journey between childhood and adulthood, has a vulnerability in common with the traveller of this parable. Whether or not there really was a real-life traveller who fell into the hands of thieves in the way that Jesus described in Luke chapter 10, we certainly know historically that the road between Jerusalem and Jericho was a dangerous one to take, and travellers on that journey would indeed often be waylaid by robbers and thieves. It may be that this was a real-life story which Jesus used to suit his purposes; it may be that Jesus made the story up as a general illustration. Either way, the point is well made: this journey is a dangerous one! And the hallmark of vulnerability belongs equally well to the adolescent.

A part of the narrative drive and parabolic content of this particular biblical story is the juxtaposition of the attitudes of the characters within the story. Apart from the traveller (our adolescent) himself, there are five groups of characters within the parable, four of whom demonstrate a wrong attitude towards the traveller and one of whom demonstrates the right one. The rightness of the Good Samaritan's response is held in stark contrast to the other four attitudes. This internal cohesion within the parable indicates to me that we are far from overstepping the boundaries of parabolic interpretation if we now give some time to investigate not only the right attitude of the Good Samaritan, but the wrong attitudes of the other four character groups.

Why is it important to examine the attitudes within this parable? If you are reading this book it is likely that you fall into one or more of the following three categories. You will either be:

a) A parent of an adolescent seeking to understand him or her better.

b) A youth leader or worker seeking to work with adolescents.

c) An adolescent yourself seeking to come to better self-understanding!

Whichever category you fall into, it is absolutely vital that we allow God by his Holy Spirit to check, test and assess our motivation when it comes to our dealings with adolescents. I want to suggest to you that as we look at the attitudes revealed in this parable, some of them may well apply to you, as indeed they have to me. I want to ask you to be ruthlessly honest in allowing the Holy Spirit to speak to you concerning your motivations, both good and bad. It is only when we understand and come to terms with what our driving passions and motivations are that we can be real before God and give him a handle on our lives and characters. Then if there are adjustments which need to be made, sins which need to be repented of and attitudes which need to be corrected, we are in a better place to allow God by his Holy Spirit to bring grace, forgiveness, wisdom, patience and equipping. So, will you please read this chapter with an open heart and ask the Holy Spirit to apply to you what needs to be applied in order to make you cleaner and purer in heart, in attitude and in motive when it comes to your (and my!) dealings with adolescents?

The first attitude in the parable itself is that of the thieves (verse 30). Obviously, to the thieves the traveller was there solely for the purposes of exploitation. I imagine that as they hid in the bushes at the side of the road and eyed their potential victim, their minds were ranging on the size of the purse he was carrying, whether he was armed or not and could therefore defend himself, the quality of his clothing and how strong he looked in terms of being able to put up a fight. They certainly wouldn't be giving any thought to their victim as an individual, nor to the effect of their behaviour upon his life (or, indeed death!) – from the thieves' perspective he existed for their benefit and for their exploitation.

Now it is possible to hold the same attitude, even subconsciously, towards adolescents. It is easy to group young people into one amorphous mass, to stereotype their attitudes and behaviour, and to capitalise on their vulnerability in terms of finance, peer group pressure, sexual identity and fashion in ways which no other age group (including old age pensioners) has to suffer.

I can think of the unemployed seventeen-year-old who was asked to do the weekly cleaning of his church in East London for a pittance as he would do it better, cheaper, and, through the necessity of unemployment, more gratefully than any of the other church members. Or my mind turns to a sixteen-year-old who, through a youth group, was enticed into pornographic photographic sessions run by two of the youth group leaders, eventually leaving behind a broken family and much psychological, emotional and spiritual scarring through this form of sexual exploitation.

I could take you to amusement arcades whose very layout is designed to exploit the vulnerability of young people, with cheaper video games at the front of the shop to draw in and entice young people towards the more expensive (and addictive) gambling machines towards the rear of the shop. Living as I do in a seaside town, in 1986 I made a particular study of gambling addiction and amusement arcades and their influence on young people. I soon discovered that the exploitation of young people operates on different levels when it comes to those arcades. One level of exploitation aims at the tendency for young people to 'bunk off' school, thus exacerbating the growing problem of truancy in this country.

Or there's the exploitation of young people's need for fun, adventure and the adrenaline boost of playing against a machine, with the inherent dangers of addiction which seems statistically to strike young people harder when it comes to 'fruit machines'. This is not least because of the adolescents' limited social opportunities, their inadequacies, peer group pressure, the desire for more money and the need to experience the adrenaline surge of the 'immediate buzz'.

There is also in some cases the exploitation of the unemployed. I came across a case where an unemployed young person was employed by a local amusement arcade but was paid his wages in tokens which could only be used to operate the machines in those arcades. And of course, in turn amusement arcades themselves become the target for other individuals seeking to exploit the young – so that in many cases we found young people being commissioned by adults to 'steal to order' in order to gain money to play machines, or to sell their sexual favours at £5 a time down by the pier, in order to feed the machines. The exploitation of youth through drug abuse was also an observable factor in some of these amusement arcades, again because, for a variety of reasons we will investigate later in the book, it is often easier to get *young* people hooked on soft drugs, and drug 'pushers' will always exploit those who give them ready returns. It was horrifying enough in statistical analysis around the local schools to discover that eleven- to fourteen-year-olds were spending in excess of £7,000 a month between them on fruit machine gambling.

I have drawn out a few isolated incidents where I have observed this attitude of exploitation in action. You, no doubt, will be able to furnish your own examples. It may however be that some of them are rather more subtle. For example, the underlying motive behind some youth work is to provide organisations with a cheap, large and willing task force for activities such as fund-raising or social action. I am convinced that what drives a number of church works is 'survival mentality' rather than kingdom expansion, and 'survival mentality' is certainly exploitative. This occurs when a church wants or seeks to obtain a successful youth work for dubious motives such as the need for the church to survive and 'maintain its witness'. Or for that church to be seen to be successful. Even some church 'family services' are little more than youth exploitation, serving sometimes as a palliative to stop youth groups being as radical as they ought to be, and as a 'damage limitation exercise' to stop older congregations being as challenged as they ought to be. The attitude of exploitation rears its ugly head where we treat individual young people or youth groups as essentially a resource pool, or a means to an end, rather than investing them with individual and group dignity, and identity. And wherever and however exploitation emerges, it is certainly a wrong attitude.

The second attitude in the parable is that of the priest and the Levite in verses 31 and 32. The point in the story is made twice, presumably for emphasis, hence, not only the priest but also a Levite (the 'spiritual' and the 'super spiritual'!) demonstrating the same wrong attitude. To the priest and to the Levite, the traveller seems to have been little more than a nuisance. Again, it's not difficult to imagine the scene, as the priest and Levite scurried by with their noses in the air and eyes averted from the bleeding mess at the side of the road opposite them. It's almost as though they are mentally consulting their Filofaxes as they scurry on their way to some important religious meeting, determined not to be interrupted by the needs of any individual.

It is not difficult for adolescents with their emotional, financial and social demands and inconveniences to quickly provoke the attitude in us that they are basically little more than a nuisance. The more set in our agendas we as adults/parents/youth workers become, the easier it is to become irritated by young people who will not fit the mould. In the parable, Jesus seems to be taking the opportunity to yet again portray the arrogance and hypocrisy of the religious. The contrast is between the outward show and the inward reaction. Young people with their refreshing dislike and disregard for religion and ritual will often therefore highlight in our attitudes and reactions any areas of religion or hypocrisy which we are indulging. Certainly, in the parable the traveller did just that for the priest and the Levite, and I suggest that our adolescent traveller will often highlight religion and hypocrisy in our lives too. When we treat the adolescent as a nuisance he is doing just that. The attitude betrays itself in phrases like, 'Two years in the army would do the youth of today the world of good!' The same attitude lies behind the angry political and media reactions towards recent street riots in our British cities, apportioning the blame at the feet of the young people (who certainly are often the perpetrators) without looking beyond the symptoms to the root causes. But I suggest it is more insidious than that.

Could it be that much of our outmoded thinking on Sunday Schools, for example, is motivated more by the subconscious concept that young people are not really where the action is at? That to have young people present throughout a church meeting is really rather inconvenient and something of a nuisance, and therefore it is best to get them out of the way? I know we would never rationalise it like that, but the examination of our actions and motives is worthwhile and can be sobering. Treating the young person who is between childhood and adulthood as basically a nuisance is not only to forget our own past, but is also shortsighted for the future, can betray religion, inflexibility and hypocrisy, and according to this parable, is certainly a wrong attitude.

Let me skip over a few verses to verse 35 so that we can examine the attitude of the innkeeper. Now I do hope I do this character no disservice, and if, when I get to heaven, I discover this was a true story and I have misjudged the man, I will do my apologising there. Certainly, I can't help thinking that there are particular characters in Scripture who consistently get a raw deal! For example, if you had been caught in major sin and then, face-to-face, been forgiven by Jesus Christ and told by him to sin no more, the chances are that from there on you would do just that. I imagine that to be the case with the woman we read about in John's Gospel, chapter 8, so it does seem rather unfortunate that for the rest of human history she continues to be referred to as 'the woman caught in adultery'! Can you imagine meeting her in heaven and saying 'Aha! so *you're* the woman caught in adultery!' A bit tough on her, don't you think? The disciple Thomas seems to have got an equally rough ride. Although it was only the one incident (and a very understandable one at that), he will forever be known as 'Doubting Thomas'. What a nickname to carry into eternity!

So I realise I *may* be doing the innkeeper an injustice, but there are not many publicans I can think of who, if given a blank cheque, would not be able to fill it in and add several noughts on to the end of the amount! Yet in effect that is what the Good Samaritan gives to this innkeeper. I suspect that, to the innkeeper, the traveller in the story was nothing more than a paying customer. And when it comes to our attitude to living with or working with young people, we need to be ruthless in rooting this out as a motivation, ie, 'What returns am I getting from this?' There is something about the vulnerability of young people and their ultimate reliance on older people which can stimulate in many youth workers the unhelpful attitude of 'need to be needed'. Many adults are involved in youth work because they are unable to form stable relationships on a peer level with other adults. Or because they crave the adulation/hero worship/reliance that young people can give them. Or because they are seeking to recapture and relive their own youth. Or need the kudos/recognition/ authority which youth work may give them. This is as true in the church scene as it is in secular youth work. As you let the Holy Spirit examine your own motives, please don't get confused over this issue – it is a good thing to enjoy working with young people but it is a bad thing if you *need* to. The difference is between whether you are *called* to do it or *driven* to do it.

Sometimes this motivation is betrayed by our reactions when we feel we are not getting the recognition due to us from young people. That is when we start talking about 'unappreciative youth'. We resent the lack of praise/credit/ thanks given for the effort we put into Friday night's club. We feel hard done by when the individual whom we were discipling actually does a runner on us and on God. Our reaction is too extreme when our son/daughter's response to our hard-planned outing is, 'It's all right,' or, 'I'm bored,' instead of wild enthusiasm. These reactions can be the tell-tale signs to our inner motivation, and again this 'What returns am I getting?' attitude is a wrong one.

Before we identify the only correct response to the traveller in the story, there is a fourth attitude, which actually prompts the whole scenario, and that is the attitude of the lawyer. We are told that he was an expert in the law. It is evident from Jesus' response that he had a good grasp of the summary of the law (verse 27). But then we have that telling phrase in verse 29 that the lawyer wanted to 'justify himself'. It is my feeling that to the lawyer, the traveller was little more than an abstract problem. It is important to know that Jewish experts in the law were able to do a kind of 'double think', which meant that they could mentally assent to the need to love God with every fibre of their being, because of who God is and what God does, and yet for this still to remain on the level of a theoretical, philosophical concept rather than a personal love relationship with God. It is this dimension of care and of relationship that Jesus is trying to elicit from the lawyer by telling the parable. Finally, at the end of the story, it is care and relationship that Jesus commands from the lawyer in verse 37. We don't know if the lawyer got there in the end, but we do know that the question that prompted the story was an attempt at self-justification.

It is possible that you could buy (and even read!) a book like this because you want a better set of abstract theories in dealing with adolescents. It's possible that you might attend a Brainstormers weekend because you want a file of information on effective youth programming. You might become an expert in understanding the etymological and sociological derivations of adolescence, and come to thoroughly understand its psychological, emotional, physical and relational development. And yet in all of this you might miss the very heartbeat of God and of the individual adolescent, and if that were the case then you and I would be missing out. And that's the fourth wrong attitude – treating adolescents as abstract problems. For ultimately adolescents are God-crafted unique individuals, beloved of him and highly valued, as we will see in the next chapter.

The fifth and final attitude revealed in the story which Jesus tells is that of the Good Samaritan, and of course this is the only correct attitude. To get the full weight of the point Jesus is making, it is necessary to understand a little of the background history between the Jews and the Samaritans. In Old Testament biblical times, Samaria was both an area and a fortified city, and because of its strategic importance it was not infrequently under attack. The Assyrians, or Arameans, waged a particularly effective siege against Samaria which you can read about in 2 Kings chapters 6 and 7.

The Arameans (who always sound like an after-shave to me!) were particularly war-like people whose technique in warfare was extremely savage. Having successfully besieged a city, they would raze its walls to the ground, kill most of the men and make slaves of the rest, and leave behind a deposit of their own soldiers to inter-marry with the remaining women. The rationale was that never again would that city either be able to, or want to, rise up against the Arameans. Through frequent attacks in a troubled history, Samaria had at times been conquered, and inter-marriage had taken place, false gods had been worshipped even to the point of child sacrifice, and in the eyes of many orthodox Hebrews, the Samaritans were a tainted race. Not only that, but those Jews who had remained faithful to Yahweh had set up an alternative worship centre on top of a mountain in Samaria (hence the question of the woman at the well of Samaria in John chapter 4), and jealousy and tension had arisen between Jerusalem and Samaria because of this. The Samaritans and the Jews therefore had no love lost between them, and it is with this historical background that Jesus makes the startling point about the right attitude of the Good Samaritan in this parable.

The attitude of the Good Samaritan in verses 33 to 35 is exemplary. It is clear that the Samaritan too was on a specific journey, and therefore one assumes that this break in his plans was as inconvenient as it might have been to the priest and the Levite. Nonetheless, the Samaritan accommodates the inconvenience. And so, at personal cost to his timetable and his pocket, the Samaritan provides the traveller with rescue, help, love, healing and finances. Not only did the Samaritan's attitude prompt action, it prompted further follow-up (verse 35). The two silver coins of verse 35 were two Greek denarii which would be approximately two days' wages, or at today's average rate, about £100. And this, moreover, with the promise of more if needed.

The implication is clear from Jesus' teaching. The correct motive is one of compassion, of care born out of developing relationship. An attitude which is prepared to spend time, money and effort at the cost of personal inconvenience in order to do the best by the traveller. You and I, in our dealings with our 'neighbours' will not infrequently find ourselves surrounded by travellers who are on a journey between childhood and adulthood, which is the Oxford English Dictionary's definition of adolescents. The question and the challenge to you and me is, 'Will we have the right attitude?' It is a mistake to wait until our motives are entirely pure before we begin to work with and for God. It is certainly true that God can best direct a moving object rather than a stationary one! The lesson for us then is that we get moving in our loving of and working with adolescents, and that it is whilst we are serving them, training, releasing and developing them, that God will make the necessary adjustments to our attitudes and motivations.

Enough to say at this stage that you and I will almost certainly need such adjustments if we are to embrace God's heart, his motives and attitudes towards young people, which leads us neatly to the next chapter: How does God feel about adolescents?

CHAPTER FOUR

THE HEARTBEAT OF GOD

– GOD'S ATTITUDE

It was Francois-Marie Arouet, more commonly known as Voltaire (1694–1778) who said, 'Si Dieu n'existait pas, il faudrait l'inventer' – 'If God did not exist, it would be necessary to invent him' (l'*Auteur du livre des trois imposteurs*).

It is most important when we come to examine a biblical framework which reveals the heart of God for young people, that we understand some basic creation principles. God does exist, and we didn't have to invent him. God existed before, is greater than and separate from his creation. And the Bible makes it clear that in extraordinary ways creation mirrors the image and character of its creator. We did not invent God in our image, but rather, he created us in his. Ecclesiastes chapter 3 tells us that, 'There is a time for everything, and a season for every activity under heaven' (Eccles 3:1). The seasons and the natural rhythms of nature, the ebb and flow of the tides, the endless rounds of the stars, all reflect not only the diversity of God's imagination, but also different aspects of his character. Romans chapter 1, verses 18–23, clearly teaches of a God who reveals himself through his creation but is superior to it and who forbids the worship of his creation. Scripture itself teaches us that it is acceptable to meditate upon God, his character, and God within his creation. The psalms are full of such meditations.

This goes some way towards explaining the very vivid use of imagery throughout the Old and New Testaments. There God compares his people to grasshoppers, eagles, locusts, clay pots, wheat and tares, sheep and goats, and so on. Jesus' use of stories, illustrations and visual aids (birds, vines, trees, mustard seeds) were very apposite means of communication (incarnational communication) for an agricultural society. But they were surely more than this. Jesus drew illustrations from nature because his Father did the same. Jesus and the Father did this because nature and creation reflect characteristics of an eternal God who loves to move in the lives of people in the times and seasons he created.

But what has this to do with God's heart for young people? Well, despite the scriptural balance that all of creation is now fallen (Romans chapter 8) we have to contend with the facts that:

a) We are made in God's image, and not he in ours. Some theologians in the past have placed too great an emphasis on their fear of anthropomorphism.

b) God's creation, although now fallen, seems to have been designed to reflect his character.

c) There are no fixed immutable laws governing creation other than those which God ordained in the first place.

The implications of these are that God actually *wanted* the creation of human life to involve a process of impregnation, gestation, lactation (all of which says much about the complementary roles of male and female), followed by the process of growing up. This latter process includes of course the phase of adolescence. So adolescence should not be looked upon as some kind of curse, or as a direct result of the Fall, but rather a part of the full creation ordinance. Childbirth and growth to maturity were always a part of the original pre-Fall plan, albeit involving less pain (Gen 1:28, 3:14–16). Genesis chapter 1 clearly teaches that when God made everything, he made it 'good' (Gen 1:4, 10, 12, 18, 21 and 25), but only after God made people uniquely in his image did he declare them, along with the rest of his creation, not only to be 'good' but *very good*'.

Genesis is equally clear that pre-Fall sexuality, sexual intercourse and childbearing is a blessing and that male and female were designed to complement one another within this. The word used in verse 18 of the relationship between male and female is 'helper' (in the Hebrew, *Ezer*, a word used fifteen times in the Old Testament to describe God himself, out of a total use in the Old Testament of nineteen times). This is *not* a word ever used to imply inferiority or subordination, but rather carries connotations of partnership.

So the process of creating *and* nurturing children through to adulthood (which encompasses adolescence) is a pre-Fall creation principle from the book of beginnings (the literal meaning of the word 'Genesis'), invoking male and female in partnership. And we can expect that children at every stage will therefore reflect, in their own times and seasons, some aspect of the character of their creator God. Again it should come as no surprise to us biblically when we realise that families exist because God himself is in the first place the original family, as noted in an earlier chapter.

If this line of reasoning is correct, we would expect to see it reflected in various ways in various parts of the Bible. And so we do. If people are made in the image of God, we would expect God to be interested in all people. And so he is (Jn 3:16, 2 Pet 3:9). And if God is the God of all people, then it must follow that God is the God of all ages of all people. And so he is (Lk 1:5–7, Acts 2:17, 1 Jn 2:12–14). If aspects of the character and working of God are revealed in his creation (albeit now fallen), and if his

Holy Spirit works in places, times and seasons (Mk 6:4–6, Acts 1:7–8, 2:1–4, 16:7–10), then we would expect different aspects of God to be revealed at different stages in the lives of his people – for young people to reflect one part of the character of God, and for older people to reflect an *additional* part. And as we look at many more biblical references a little later in this chapter we will see this to be the case.

All of this should serve to convince us biblically that since the beginning of creation, God has been interested in all people of all ages, all created in his image and reflecting in places, times and seasons something of the character and work of God. This allows us to understand biblically that within God's primary aim of fathering humanity there are subsets of people-groups to whom God pays particular attention. It is not that they are merely favourites, but rather that their particular place, time or season renders them particularly vulnerable, or peculiarly reflects certain aspects of God's nature. So we know that although God loves all people, he has a special place in his heart for widows and orphans (Ex 22:22, Deut 10:18, 1 Tim 5:3–5, Acts 6:1–7). We know that God has a place in his heart for the poor and oppressed (Lk 4:18–21). Similarly, for foreigners and exiles (Num 35:15, Lev 25:35). And Scripture is very clear that God also has a special place in his heart for young people, for all the reasons outlined above.

Before we look at the Bible passages on which I base the previous statement, there are two other reasons why God has a special and high regard for young people. The first concerns the church. We have said in a previous chapter that God has always been looking to incarnate his message. The supreme incarnation of the message (Word) of God was, of course, Jesus Christ, the Word made flesh. It was into Jesus that the Holy Spirit was poured without limit (John 3:34). It was after Jesus' water baptism and the descent of the Holy Spirit upon him (Mt 3:16–17) that Jesus was led by that same Holy Spirit into his first successful confrontation with the Enemy (Mt 4:1). God has always been looking for a body that will 'flesh out' his message, accomplish his will and be filled out by his Holy Spirit (in the Greek, *pneuma* – Holy Spirit, that which fills out to the correct shape from the inside, hence our word 'pneumatic').

God has not changed. After Jesus ascended to the Father he left behind him thousands of little 'Christs' who were to be drawn together to 'church it' together (in the Greek, *ecclesia* – church, a group or body of like-minded, called-out people). This church (whose precedents were Abraham's Hebraic descendants, the called-out and chosen people of God in the Old Testament) was to be the second body of Jesus Christ on earth. And like the first body, the church is to be filled with God's Holy Spirit (Acts 1:8, 2:38–39, Eph 5:18). The New Testament uses different images to capture the essence of what this church is. It is a building (1 Pet 2:4–12) because it is perpetually being added to with extensions, and the living stones are being fitted together through the cement of the love of God's Holy Spirit. It is also a body (1 Cor 12:12–27, Rom 12:4–5) because it is a living, breathing, moving organism, not an organisation. It is a bride (Rev 21:2, 9) because the church is special, beautiful, and is essentially loving and sacrificial towards the bridegroom, as is he to her. It is also a battalion (Eph 6:10–18, 2 Tim 2:3–4), because the church is a fighting unit in a fallen world order where the only kind of theology that makes sense of sin, sickness, Satan and suffering is a warfare theology, which understands the clash of two kingdoms: God's and Satan's.

But the church of Jesus Christ (who is and will always remain its head (Col 1:18, Eph 5:23, Mt 16:18) is also a family. We have already seen that families exist because God himself is family (Father, Son and Holy Spirit) and all concepts of fatherhood and of family owe their origins to the nature and character of 'Father God' (Eph 3:14–15).

This family of God is to be a prophetic demonstration to principalities and powers and to their influence here on earth, that whilst in the kingdom of God there are differing spheres of function and authority, different times and seasons within the lives of God's people which reveal different attributes of God himself, there is no room for division, disunity, racism, sexism *or* ageism. This is why the book of Ephesians teaches so clearly on the role of the individual in Christ, on the church family of the saints, on the role of husbands, wives, children and employers, and yet finishes with some of the clearest teaching on spiritual warfare that there is in the Bible. It is because relationships and family and unity and peace are an essential part of spiritual warfare, prophetically demonstrated in the church. So the second reason why God has a special place in his heart for young people is because they are an integral, vital, necessary and prophetic part of the second body of Jesus Christ on earth, his church. Real family removes the barriers (Eph 2:11–22, Gal 3:26 – 4:7).

Further evidence of the special niche that youth occupy in the heart of God lies in our understanding of the kingdom of God. It has for long been demonstrably observable that the quality of life in any given civilisation depends to some extent upon the value that that civilisation places on the lives of its children. One of the symptoms of the decline of the Roman and Greek empires was their increasingly cruel and oppressive treatment of children, ranging through abortion, abandonment, and abuse right through to child sacrifice. A society which places low value on the life of its unborn or developing children is not far from devaluing the other extremity of old age and passing a general judgement on the value of life as a whole. Legalised abortion not infrequently precedes legalised euthanasia. Such a society quickly becomes one of 'might and the majority is right', where an individual's value is based on usefulness/output/ exploitation, and where pragmatics and hedonistic existentialism replace absolutes.

It is certainly true that in biblical times many of the societies which surrounded the Hebrew people, and then in the New Testament, the Christians, placed little or no value on the life of youth. At different times in her history, Israel found herself surrounded by nations which practised abortion, the abandonment of sick, infirm or even merely female children shortly after birth, the deliberate crippling of children to provide alms, the ritualistic abuse of children in temple rites and child sacrifice. Even the enlightened Jew adopted the attitude that 'children should be seen and not heard', and the sometimes too casual mention of women and children in the New Testament Bible narratives reflect this attitude (Mt 14:21, Mk 6:44).

But the kingdom of God has a remarkable way of reversing the values of the societies that surround its inhabitants. It is in the kingdom of God that the first get to be last and vice versa (Mk 9:35). According to Jesus, the one who wants to be greatest should (significantly) become like the youngest, and the one who wants to rule should be the greatest servant (Lk 22:26). Worldly wisdom is kingdom folly (1 Cor 1:20–21). And typically, the greatest example of this kingdom reversal is, of course, Jesus himself (Jn 13). So the kingdom of God reverses the rules, and the poor in spirit receive the kingdom of heaven, the mourners are comforted, the meek inherit the earth, the persecuted are happy, and enemies are loved (Mt 5). Sinners, prostitutes and tax collectors were on the end of this reversal, which is one reason why Jesus was received by the ordinary people but rejected by the religious. Against the social norms of the time, women were treated with dignity, value and respect by Jesus (the Samaritan woman at the well, the disciples Mary and Martha, the first witnesses to the resurrection, and so on). And God's heart and dealing with children and young people similarly reverses the trends of fallen society. Where society denigrates and devalues, God raises and restores.

We can now see three reasons why God holds children

and youth dear to himself: they reveal aspects of the Godhead not so clearly seen in other parts of his creation; they are an integral part of the prophetic body of Jesus Christ on earth, the church; and they clearly indicate kingdom priorities, reversing fallen society's sinful values.

In support of the above three observations, it will now be necessary to undertake a brief biblical survey of God's attitude to youth. I urge you to look up the following references and examine them in context. It is my experience that a well-established biblical framework has all the potential of actually affecting our lives and life styles. For the parent, teacher and youth leader, the following references are therefore vital.

God and youth

We have already discovered that the Bible does recognise youth and the state of adolescence as a separate category, and this is evidenced by the differentials in taxes required to be paid by youths and adults (Lev 27). The Bible does place orphaned children alongside widows as a special category for protection (Ex 22:21–24). The worst curses that could fall upon an enemy involved the death or murder of his children (Ps 137:9), and the violent death of children was seen as a terrible calamity (Nahum 3:10). Pagan nations around Israel involved themselves in what God denounced as an abomination when they sacrificed children to such gods as Molech (Lev 20:1–5), which is one reason why God dealt so severely with the enemies of Israel in the Old Testament. And the children of Israel would know that they were under the worst of curses when they took to the abominable practice of cannibalising their own children (Lev 26:29) which actually occurred on a number of occasions (for example: 2 Kings 6 and 7 – Israel had been forewarned in Deuteronomy 28). When disaster was forecast as coming upon the nation of Israel, its terrible extent was emphasised by the way in which both young and old (the God of all ages and all extremes) would be affected (Deut 28:41, 49–50).

In contrast to this, the provision of children (particularly, in that society, male heirs) was seen as a direct blessing from God (Ps 127:3–5), and the happiness and well-being of youth was also seen as a symptom of God's favour and blessing upon a nation (Zech 8:5, 9:17).

And God's dealings in the lives of young people evidently began at the earliest of ages (Ps 139:13–16). As indeed did his specific call upon their lives and destiny (Jer 1:5–7). We are therefore not surprised to find references to Moses as a beautiful child in the eyes of God (Acts 7:20), to Samson being blessed by God in his youth (Judg 13:24), to John the Baptist being filled with the Holy Spirit whilst still in his mother's womb (Lk 1:15), or to Jesus being angelically announced as Saviour, even whilst yet a babe (Lk 2:11). Nor will we be surprised that God's attitude and heart towards youth should be that they would grow up in the knowledge and love of him, as did Samuel (1 Sam 2:21 and 26).

In order to grow in God, children and young people must of course have the right of access to him and this again is evidenced in the ministry of Jesus (Mt 19:13–15, Mk 10:13–16, Lk 18:15–17). God is at pains to speak to young people, even repeatedly where necessary (1 Sam 3:1–24), even if in so doing he has to bypass the older (Eli) and middle generations (the wicked sons of Eli) in order to get through to a thirteen- or fourteen-year-old youth (Samuel). God derives glory from the praises of children and young people (Ps 8:1–2, which Jesus quotes in his triumphal entry into Jerusalem in Matthew 21:15–16). And he sees the renewal of youth to those who are older as a good and positive thing to be desired (Ps 103:1–5). As far as God is concerned, the younger you are the greater the example you can potentially be to those who would be great in the kingdom of God (Lk 22:24–26), and it is significant that God views all of his people as children when it comes to his loving discipline (Heb 12:5–13) just as he views us all as children when it comes to receiving the gift of the Holy Spirit to produce conviction, repentance, fruit and gifts (Lk 11:11–13).

We can therefore readily see that understanding God's heart for young people is not a matter of simply plucking a few verses from Old and New Testament, but rather that this is a consistent theme that runs throughout Scripture. There is therefore a clear case to be made for God having a special place in his heart and attitude toward young people.

Advantages of youth

As is so often the case, the Bible is not content merely to state what God is like, but also why he is like that and how this works out. This is in order that, although his ways are higher than ours (Is 55:9), we might none the less come to know and love his ways and character. God *is* knowable; he is supernaturally natural and naturally supernatural. For these reasons then, the Bible goes on to *explain* some of the advantages of being young, seen mainly from God's perspective.

It is certainly an advantage to be childlike because it is children who inherit the kingdom of God (Mt 18:1–4), and the things of the kingdom previously hidden from adults have now been revealed to children (Mt 11:25–26). Each child (and presumably childlikeness) is further rewarded not only by special recognition within the kingdom of heaven, but also by the allocation of personal angelic 'minders' (Mt 18:10). And young people in the New Testament (as in the Old) are often linked to heroic feats of bravery (Acts 23:16–22, Jn 6:9). The evidence for this is great in the Old Testament, including: the heroic spies sent out into enemy territory (Josh 6:23); the youthful David successful in slaying his enemy, Goliath (1 Sam 17:33); the youthful and victorious warriors of Psalm 110 verses 1–3; and the Old Testament assurance that the strength of youth is their glory before God (Prov 20:29). According to the Old Testament, youthfulness is a cause for cheering and rejoicing, and also for remembering God (Eccles 11:9), and a positive hallmark of youth is devotion and the proclivity to follow (Jer 2:1–2). Youth was no barrier to God providing young people with wisdom beyond their years (1 Kings 3:6–14). And so the list of Old and New Testament young heroes continues to grow: Joseph; Joshua (whose Hebrew name is the equivalent of the Aramaic Jesus, both meaning 'deliverer of his people'); and Caleb (whose name significantly means 'dog-like follower', as young people are surely born to be followers), chosen at the expense of a generation making an eleven-day journey in forty years! (Another older generation, like Eli's sons, bypassed in favour of youth.) Then there's David, Solomon, Esther, Daniel, Hananiah and Mishael.

And in the New Testament: Mary, the earthly mother of Jesus (church tradition tells us she was about sixteen when she gave birth to Jesus); the boy with the loaves and fishes; Paul's nephew who warned the centurions; the writer of Mark's Gospel (probably about fifteen at the time of the events); and the favourite friend of Jesus (John – probably aged about seventeen at the time of the events); Timothy (running a resource church of about 25,000 people in his late teens); and of course Jesus himself, who had completed his earthly mission by the age of thirty-three. The New Testament avows that young men and women will prophesy and see visions (Acts 2:17), that young people can also be young in evil (1 Cor 14:20b), and that it is a symptom of youth to crave not only physical, but also spiritual food. Youth also have the advantage of growing into all that lies ahead of them in God (1 Pet 2:2).

The Bible is, of course, totally realistic and also lists some disadvantages of youth. These are often the flip-side of the coin which I have described above. Young people *are* referred to as being immature in their thinking (1 Cor

14:20a) as well as immature in the amount of teaching which they can receive (1 Cor 3:1–2). This means that their speech, their thoughts and their reasoning might also be immature (1 Cor 13:11). But it's plain to see from a comparison of these two lists where the weight of biblical example lies. After all, we have to grapple with the fact that Jesus Christ, the perfect Son of God, must also have been at some stage a teenager in perfect relationship with his Father. Of course, there is that intriguing little phrase in Luke 2:52 which talks of Jesus 'growing in favour' with God as well as with men, but whatever that means, it cannot mean that there was a time when Jesus was sinful as a child or as a teenager, as other scriptures insist that Jesus, despite being tempted in every way as we are (Hebrews 4:15), was yet without sin (2 Cor 5:21).

Minor to major

Although we can now maintain biblically that God reserves a special place in his heart and kingdom for youth, we have also seen that this will never be at the exclusion of other people groups (for some of whom he also reserves a special place). Consequently, the Bible, continuing in realistic vein, builds a framework for the relative behaviour of young people to older. So this is going to be a really good section for you to obtain a few proof texts from, should you need to fire them at your wayward adolescents! (Don't take that remark too seriously. . . .)

In Exodus 20:12 children are told to honour their mothers and fathers, and that part of the blessing resulting from this will be a long life and a full inheritance (which doesn't just mean the family silver!). Leviticus 19:32 further expands this and talks about youth honouring older people in general. You find a similar extension in the New Testament where Ephesians 6:1–3 talks about children obeying and honouring their parents (as does Colossians 3:20), and then 1 Peter 5:5 widens the element of youth submitting to older people in general, whilst then going on to stress that we are *all* to be humble towards one another, presumably irrespective of age. There will, however, come occasions when young people ought and will be equipped to exhort or even rebuke their elders, and the Bible then indicates how that should be done (1 Tim 5:1), whilst encouraging young people not to hold back (Jer 1:6–7) and commanding them not to allow older people to look down on them because of their youth (1 Tim 4:12).

Major to minor

But before you get *too* excited about how young people ought to relate to you, have a look at how the Bible builds a framework for *our* behaviour towards them! We are certainly to involve young people in family life and worship (Lk 2:41–52, with perhaps an inherent warning not to lose them along the way!) Parents are commanded in particular not to exasperate or to embitter and therefore discourage their children (Eph 6:4, Col 3:21). And an illustration of Jesus' clearly highlights an expectation that parents will give good gifts to their children (Lk 11:11–13). We are clearly told as adults that young people can be an example to us (Tit 2:3–8) and that we are therefore to be prepared to receive them as from God (1 Cor 16:10–11). If young people are commanded by God not to allow older people to look down on them because of their youth, then certainly the command cuts both ways and we as adults are forbidden to look down on young people merely because of the age differential (1 Tim 4:12).

So there you have it: a biblical framework for understanding God's heart and attitude towards young people. If it is his heart and attitude, it should and can also be ours (1 Pet 1:15–16). We have seen the advantages and the disadvantages of being young, and can begin to understand that many of these advantages can be transferred to older people too. This is because God's gifting and calling is irrevocable (Rom 11:29) and God therefore wants to add strings to our bow, not take them away from us. So to our strength, zealousness, faithfulness, devotion and willingness to follow that goes with youth, God wants to add the wisdom, patience and experience of age, not swap one for the other!

And finally we have seen how the Bible recommends that younger people should treat older, and vice versa. This information must now find its way from our heads (Hos 4:6) to our hearts (Prov 29:18), in order that the information alone will not lead us into frustration, but rather that God's revelation will lead to the transformation of our hearts and attitudes towards young people.

CHAPTER FIVE

THEM AND US?

– EXTERNAL PRESSURES ON ADOLESCENTS

It has been my experience whilst working with young people, both in the education system in this country and abroad, and also in various youth groups and activities (both secular and Christian), that we can make a valid generalisation to help us understand the different phases that the adolescent grows through on his journey from childhood to adulthood.

The first phase covers eleven- to fourteen-year-olds, when external social pressure is strong to produce the formation of gangs, an impulse stronger within boys than girls, though it is observable in both. These gangs tend to be single sex. They are often led by strong characters, though the strength may lie more in their muscles than in their personality! There is a fair amount of expressed antipathy between the sexes at this stage. Boys see girls as 'soppy', kissing as a kind of masculine sell-out to the male gang, and co-ordinated attempts by the gangly adolescent at such social interaction as dancing, as being at best, embarrassing. On the other hand, most girls at this age would voice the opinion (if not hold it in private) that boys are immature, aggressive, bad mannered and loutish.

It is again a generalisation, but often found to be true, that gangs of girls will hold together more out of a sense of belonging and friendship, whereas the male equivalent will be held together more by function and common interest, for example, membership of a youth group, a football team, BMX bikes, or territorial squabbling.

Such gangs and gang leaders command great loyalty and have the power to project their social mores (both good and bad) into the lives of the individual gang members. Loyalty is a key word during this phase of adolescent development, and 'splitting' or 'dobbing' on gang members is regarded as the ultimate betrayal, with the probable consequence of social ostracism.

It is important to note that as the adolescent begins to understand how group dynamics work, and sociologists inform us that this phase of gang mentality is vital to future social development, he or she will also be experimenting with the parameters of perceived authority. It is not true that most of the under-fourteen-year-olds are actively rebelling against authority at this stage; rather, they are testing it to see how far they can go. Most parents will recognise this phase early on in the life of their children when at the age of about eighteen months to two years the child will wilfully test the parameters placed around it, be that the hour at which it should be in bed, or the number of times that Mum or Dad will pick up a rattle thrown from the pram. The object is to chart the boundaries of parental (or other) authority figures. As we seek to understand in this chapter how many of such boundaries society has actively dismantled, thereby doing the developing adolescent a great disservice, we will come to realise how important it is that boundaries and parameters of authority are both set, adhered to and *explained*.

The second phase of adolescent development occurs in the fifteen- to sixteen-year-old bracket. This period is frequently called the transition stage as it marks the phase of adolescence between the homosexual stage and the later heterosexual stage. In the former the adolescent will spend much of his or her time with the same sex, and there may actually be homosexual attraction and experimentation in an attempt to establish and validate the adolescent's own sexuality, and in a search for acceptable role models. In the later heterosexual stage the adolescent's attention is focused mainly on the opposite sex. During this transitional phase between the two stages of sexual attraction the gangs tend to break down into smaller cliques, as the adolescent attempts to discover greater emotional (and sometimes physical) intimacy with a friend. Usually this confiding of secrets, sharing of problems and comparison of experiences is with a friend of the same sex. As much of the discussion centres around sexuality (for reasons we will look at in the next chapter), it is often within these same-sex cliques that attitudes are formed regarding relationships and approach to sexuality. The move from the gang mentality to the clique mentality is often marked by a rejection of the former gang, since in the eye of the developing adolescent, that would now be seen as being childish.

It should also be noted that the fifteen- to sixteen-year-old phase often involves a wilful decision either to reject the parameters and boundaries set around the adolescent, or more or less to co-operate with that authority. This is one of the reasons why this age range is notoriously the most difficult to teach in schools (fourth and fifth years), although there are other external social pressures at work in the school, for example, the imminence of exams, and, after school, the pressure of possible long-term unemployment.

By the time the adolescent reaches the sixteen to twenty-one phase, the cliques have broken down still further into one-to-one exclusive relationships, most usually male to female. This is beyond the transitional stage and is into the heterosexual stage of adolescence, and is marked initially by social dating, where the main aim is to enjoy the company of the opposite sex and to assess the ability of the adolescent to attract the opposite sex. Ongoing adjustment in these relationships is caused by adolescents refining their understanding of the qualities they are looking for in a partner of the opposite sex, as they move out of the phase of the adolescent crush (which belongs more to the fifteen- to sixteen-year-old phase) and into the more exclusive heterosexual relationships of the sixteen- to twenty-one-year-old phase. This experimentation will, however, sometimes earn for the adolescent the term 'flirt'. From about eighteen onwards, the adolescent is much more interested in the formation of a 'steady' partnership. During this phase of adolescent development most life attitudes will have been formed, which is why classically this age at school (the sixth form) is very good at debates on Christianity, but it's extremely difficult to get them to change their minds. This is because whilst attitudes have been formed concerning what life is about and what the adolescent wants out of it, there has not been sufficient time for experience to test out the attitudes taken, and therefore this stage of adolescence is marked by both idealism and a lack of perspective.

Whilst avoiding the dangers of seeking to place individual adolescents whom we know into the categories outlined above, there is sufficient truth contained in them for them to be a helpful guideline. However, there is a common factor which runs across the three phases of adolescent development and that is the external pressure which society places upon adolescents at *every* stage of their growth. If adolescence is an age of causes (and it is) then one of the key pressures which society places upon the adolescent is in the removal of all absolutes, thereby denying the real meaning and value of any causes. Humanity has achieved greater technological and scientific advancements during the course of my lifetime than it has in all of the centuries preceding it. In the western world, we now live in an instant consumerised and trivialised society. Change has been with us throughout the generations, but the rate of change is accelerating enormously, with the result that humanity is hurled headlong into a society where that which does not change is inconceivable, where absolutes (God, the Bible, right and wrong) are inadmissible, where the god of science has failed (pollution, the nuclear threat) yet still holds sway, and where therefore what we experience in the present is all important. The past retreats with increasing irrelevance, and the future holds, at best, uncertainty, and at worst, impending doom. It is in this social climate that the philosophy of existentialism has gathered populist support, where what you can experience predetermines what actually *is*. The results of such destabilisation are, for the adolescent, very marked.

In such a society there is little room for absolutes, for boundaries and parameters, and commitment to a cause (be that the peace movement, anti-vivisection, or even God) is hard to elicit and seems to have little meaning. The external social pressures which face adolescents today are like the wind and waves of arbitrary change, with no sense of purpose or direction, the result being that the adolescent is cast adrift on a sea of doubt. And this, at a time when explained and reasonable barriers and boundaries are most needed, is society's grave disservice to the adolescent. It is a disservice which we, the church, cannot afford to emulate, as did the liberal church of the post-war years.

Let's take a break here and have a look at the following diagram.

As the adolescent develops, there are a series of internal strains, tensions, pressures and conflicts which go on within him or her. I have marked these internal areas of change, noted in chapter one, in the form of five arrows within the figure in the diagram. Each arrow represents one life-related area of change in the adolescent. We are informed by sociologists that potentially there are five key times of stress in the life of every individual. These are times when external circumstances react with internal

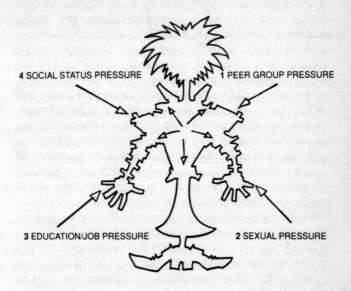

4 SOCIAL STATUS PRESSURE

1 PEER GROUP PRESSURE

3 EDUCATION/JOB PRESSURE

2 SEXUAL PRESSURE

pressures to provide prominent times of stress and tension. These have been identified as marriage, change of job (or loss of job), change of house, bereavement, and birth of a child. What is often overlooked, however, is that these five key stress points usually occur in the life of the adult. It remains true to say that for most people, at no time other than adolescence do *all* of our internal life-related areas change to the same extent at the same time.

It's important to look at the external pressures which I have indicated in the diagram above with arrows pointed at the figure from the outside. At the very time when all of this turmoil is going on *within* the life of the adolescent, society, having eradicated most absolutes and parameters, then goes on to inflict external pressure in four key ways.

The first is through peer group pressure, exerted not only

by other adolescents, but also by those bodies (fashion houses, and the music, communications and media industries) which fish from the relatively affluent adolescent pool. Secondly, there is sexual pressure on the adolescent as the age of sexual consent lies right in the middle of adolescence (sixteen years), whilst the age for legal marriage with parental permission is the same, and without permission only two years later, at eighteen years. Thirdly, most education or job pressure is exerted during the adolescent years, with life decisions having to be made by adolescents or imposed upon them by parents and teachers concerning future education, the choice of possible job and training schemes that may go with that, or the prospects of short, medium, or long-term unemployment. Fourthly, there is the external pressure of what I call social status. Again, society is doing the adolescent no favours by throwing into the mix the legal possibility of a full driving licence at seventeen, the legal consumption of alcohol under all circumstances at eighteen, the right to vote for the political future of this country at eighteen, and the right to buy cigarettes at sixteen. This is not an argument merely for deferring these external pressure points, but rather a plea that we better understand these pressures at the crucial time that they arrive.

We can now see that the pressures faced by adolescents are not all internal, but are exacerbated by external social pressures. These produce a plethora of anomalies as the transfer of privilege and responsibility, with its attendant tensions and pressures in western society, is not only gradual, but often unhelpful! For example

Ten-year-old	– responsible for criminal offences
Thirteen-year-old	– can be employed for light work
Fourteen-year-old	– can go in a pub (but not buy alcohol)
Fifteen-year-old	– can open a Giro account

Sixteen-year-old — can leave school
— can hold a driving licence for a moped
— can work a forty-eight hour week
— can buy tobacco
— can buy wine and beer with meals
— can consent to medical treatment
— can get married with parental consent
— girls can consent to sexual intercourse

Seventeen-year-old — can go into betting shops (but not bet)
— can become street traders
— can hold an ordinary driving licence

Eighteen-year-old — the age of majority (parents no longer legally responsible)
— can get married without parental consent
— Can drink alcohol in pubs and clubs
— can watch adult films
— can place bets
— can make legal contracts
— can be sent to an ordinary prison
— can be tattooed
— can vote

Twenty-one-year-old — can become an MP
— can adopt a child
— can consent to homosexual practices

You can see by this list that it takes some eleven years

to become an 'adult' in the fully legal sense of the word in Britain today. The social pressures attendant upon this are enormous. Before we move in the subsequent chapters from the external to the internal pressures, I would like to conclude this chapter with a brief statistical overview of the results of some of these social pressures on the lives of adolescents.

Some thirty per cent of the world's six billion population is under the age of twenty, some fifty per cent is under the age of twenty-two, and a staggering sixty per cent is under the age of twenty-four – which means that a phenomenal amount of adolescents particularly in the West are feeling the very pressures we have just identified! Let's take a look at some of the social pressures attendant upon adolescents in that great bastion of teenage and youth culture, the United States of America.

In the last twenty minutes whilst you have been reading this book twenty-nine teenagers have attempted suicide, fifty-seven have left home, there have been fourteen teenage illegitimate births, whilst a further twenty-two teenagers under the age of nineteen have had abortions. Many of America's drug problems, particularly among young people, have now been exported to the UK, but in America the problem remains huge. In the last thirty minutes, 685 teenagers who already have a drug problem have taken more drugs, 188 adolescents have been involved in a serious abuse of alcohol over that same period of time, whilst there have been an additional 286 victims of broken homes, plus 228 beaten or molested – physically or sexually – by their parents. And against this backdrop, seventy-nine per cent of American parents said that they were in good communication with their children, whilst eighty-one per cent of those same teenage children said that communication was poor or non-existent.

Before we pat ourselves on the back in our parochialism and thank God for the Atlantic, the situation is little better in the UK. Whereas in the USA approximately one in two weddings end in divorce, in the UK that statistic is one in three. And this means that one in five of today's youth will see their home break up before the age of sixteen years. The UK is currently producing some 160,000 teenagers a year from recently broken homes. At the same time, the number of illegitimate children has doubled over the last twenty years and now stands at one in four. By the mid-1980s the National Society for Prevention of Cruelty to Children was dealing with more than 37,000 cases of suspected injury, youth at risk, cases of neglect, abandonment, sexual abuse and marital failure.

Over a twenty-year period from the late 1960s juvenile crimes of violence more than quadrupled, and it is now unfortunately true that more than fifty per cent of all indictable crime is committed by people under the age of twenty-five years. During the last ten years of that period (1977–1987) the highest rate of offending was among males aged between fourteen and under seventeen (7,400 per 100,000 of the population). The second highest was among males aged between seventeen and under twenty-one (7,100 per 100,000 of the population). These crime statistics break down as follows. People under the age of twenty committed: forty-five per cent of all crimes of violence against a person; thirty-five per cent of all sexual offences; sixty-eight per cent of all burglary; fifty-eight per cent of all robbery; and fifty-eight per cent of all theft and handling. Twenty-year-olds and under committed: twenty-eight per cent of all fraud and forgery; sixty per cent of all criminal damage; twenty-seven per cent of all drug offences; twenty-five per cent of motoring offences; and thirty-five per cent of all other indictable offences. In the mid-1980s, fifteen years was the peak age for male offenders, whilst fourteen years was the peak age of all female offenders. At that time in one year there were approximately 20,000 teenagers in youth custody, with a further 12,000 in police detention.

In later chapters we will examine some statistics more

specifically connected with the internal areas of interrelated change (physical, emotional, mental, social, spiritual). Meanwhile, these statistics and this brief overview do paint a grim picture of society at large and the way that it fails to meet the needs of the developing adolescent. In a world of turmoil, change and insecurity, you and I as Christian parents, youth leaders, teachers and youth workers *can* learn and understand what is going on inside adolescents and we *can* see God's Holy Spirit so fill them with the breath of God (remember, that that's from the Greek, *pneuma* – that which fills from the inside to the correct shape) that they are able to withstand the external pressures from a faltering society around them.

CHAPTER SIX

LET'S GET PHYSICAL

– THE PHYSICAL DEVELOPMENT OF THE ADOLESCENT

'I would there were no age between ten and three-and-twenty, or that youth would sleep the rest.'

Shakespeare

'Young men have strong passions and tend to gratify them indiscriminately. Of bodily desires, it is by the sexual that they are most easily swayed and in which they show an absence of self-control.'

Aristotle

It is perhaps in the area of physical change that the clearest signals are given, both to adolescents and to the world around them, of the onset of adolescence. Physical change and development is often summed up in the word 'puberty', though it is important to note that physical changes are by no means restricted to sexuality. However, since it is estimated that sexuality is the uppermost thing in the mind of every adolescent, occurring to him or her approximately once every fourteen minutes (!), it is important to spend a fair amount of time in this chapter examining the implications of puberty upon the adolescent.

It is true that the onslaught of puberty varies not only by age, but also by sex and indeed by culture. The necessary release of sexual hormones, stimulated by the pituitary gland at the base of the brain and by the reproductive organs (ovaries in females, testes in males), is affected by a variety of circumstances, some internal (the overall physical rate of development in the individual) and some external (stress, diet, and even expectations of society surrounding the individual). So it was that in Victorian society, where girls were shorter and lighter, the beginning of menstruation for females was approximately at the age of sixteen. Modern western society, with an improvement in diet and therefore taller and heavier girls, has brought this down to the age of approximately 10–12 years. For the male adolescent, the age at which puberty begins for most males in western cultures is at approximately eleven or twelve years, though there is some evidence to indicate that it is slightly earlier for eastern cultures.

These general trends serve to explain an interesting observation which can be made of most schools in our country. In the first and second years at school (eleven and twelve years old) most girls not only look more mature than boys of their age, but are actually physically larger in many cases, although males from eastern cultures at that age often appear to be a little ahead of the development scale, particularly in terms of facial hair and broken voices.

By pursuing this staggered developmental process to its logical conclusion (whereby girls begin puberty a year or two ahead of males on average) we can also come to an understanding of why, in general, most males are larger in stature than most females. If a male and female child are born on the same date, their average growth and physical development will be at the same rate up until the beginning of puberty – for the girl, at about the age of ten. Then with the release of sex hormones and the beginning of menstruation, the girl will go through a very rapid growth spurt. This is not the first she will have experienced, but it is the first which is out of synchronisation with that experienced by her male counterpart. This means that in the growth stakes she now pulls considerably ahead of the male, and so around the age of ten, eleven, twelve and even thirteen, will have grown somewhat larger than her male counterpart in physical stature. The process of physical maturity as well as physical growth will also mean that she will tend to behave more 'adult' than her male counterpart.

In the meanwhile, the male continues to develop at the pre-pubescent rate which is somewhat slower. Then, with the onslaught of puberty, for him in general at the age of eleven or twelve, he goes through an enormous growth spurt. But the difference now is that his growth spurt is on top of an additional one or two years' steady growth which the girl never got, which means that by the end of the male's pubescent growth spurt, he will in general have overtaken the female's physical development in stature, which is one way of accounting for the fact that most males are bigger in stature than females.

For the female, puberty marks the beginning of menstruation, which can be a physically and emotionally traumatic time, particularly without the educative and helpful support of parents and teachers to provide a normative role model. Often for the girl there is a mixture of fear and embarrassment that menstruation and a changing body can bring. Not only will the menstrual cycle start and eventually become regular; puberty for the female also marks the development of fatty tissues in and around the body, particularly at the hips, thighs, buttocks and breasts in preparation for childbirth.

For the male there is often no such easily identifiable start to the process of puberty, but the changes that occur obviously include the settling of the voice usually to a lower pitch, which may be accompanied by uncontrollable vocal inflections, ranging from embarrassing high pitched squeaks to lower deep down growls! Fatty tissue in the male's body will often be replaced by muscles, and the early adolescent will then lose much of his 'puppy fat'. For both the male and the female there will be a marked growth of body hair, though this is generally more marked and more observable in the male than in the female. This body hair will be of a coarser nature than the fine downy hair found on most pre-pubescents and will develop on the legs and under the arms of the male and female, and for the male in addition sometimes on his chest and on the face and neck. For the male, external genital development is also marked with a lengthening and filling out of both the penis and the testicles, with hair developing on both the male and female in the genital areas also. The closest male equivalent to the female onset of menstruation is an increased capacity (actually present in some forms since babyhood) for penile erection, production of sperm and now also for ejaculation. This will often take the form initially of nocturnal emissions or so-called 'wet dreams', and will later most probably also involve masturbation.

The body will reach its physical peak at around the age of seventeen years, and in the male its peak for sexual capacity (in terms of energy and procreative capacity) at about the age of eighteen years. It is small wonder that in the face of such dramatic, relatively sudden and enormous bodily changes, sex and sexuality is uppermost in the mind of most adolescents.

We have already made the point that it is impossible and artificial to segregate the interrelated areas of change in the life of any adolescent, and it will now readily be seen that the areas of physical change will quickly impinge upon the social, recreational and emotional areas of development in that same adolescent. The young person who has previously enjoyed games and PE at school may now become acutely embarrassed at the thought of the communal shower room, where much furtive glancing and embarrassed comparisons will take place concerning the development of female breasts or the length of the penis!

The lad who quickly develops body hair on genitals, legs and neck (usually before face) will become acutely and embarrassedly aware that he is hairy as other lads might not be, and will wish that he were otherwise. At the same time, those guys who remain as smooth-skinned as they were before puberty will often taunt their hirsute companion from a basis of secret insecurity and envy. The lad who begins shaving at eleven will be living with the tension of pride that he needs to do so, and embarrassment that his neck bears the evidence of the scars!

Such dramatic changes of the bodies of adolescents, aided and abetted by the upsurge of chemical sex hormones, and surrounded by the external pressures of media (provocative and seductive fashion, explicit magazines with youth problem pages, and readily obtainable pornographic videos and magazines) all lead to an understandable tendency towards experimentation. If we, like the men of Issachar, are to understand fully the times in which we live and know how to respond (1 Chron 12:32) then it will be necessary to take a brief statistical survey of available information giving us an insight into the nature and extent of this sexual experimentation, as well as behavioural trends.

In 1990, a national newspaper conducted a confidential survey among more than 1,100 teenagers concerning their lifestyle, attitudes and morals. The poll, whilst not exhaustive, was certainly revealing in the general trends it indicated. One of the newspaper banner headlines read: 'One in three teenagers have sex by the age of sixteen' (the importance of the age sixteen being, of course, that it is the age of legal consent). The survey revealed that one third of girls are no longer virgins by the time they reach eighteen. More than ten per cent of the teenagers surveyed had experienced sexual intercourse by the age of fourteen, with ten per cent of girls aged thirteen and fourteen, and thirteen per cent of boys of the same age claiming that they had already had sexual intercourse. By the time the adolescent reached fifteen and sixteen years, the percentages had risen to a total of twenty-nine per cent of girls and thirty-five per cent of boys having had sexual intercourse.

The statistics related to the UK and had some interesting regional variations. It seemed that teenagers in the Midlands were the most promiscuous (with four out of ten having intercourse by the age of eighteen, compared with thirty-two per cent in the south and thirty-one per cent in Scotland and the north). There was also some indication of class/environmental differentiation: twenty-five per cent of teenagers from detached homes had had intercourse by the age of sixteen compared with forty-six per cent from terraced homes. And the overall survey indicated that over the thirteen to eighteen age range, thirty-six per cent of boys had had sexual intercourse by the age of eighteen, compared with thirty-two per cent of girls.

There are interesting comparisons between these figures and those produced by a survey commissioned across 150 church youth groups from around the UK dealing with information given by thirteen- to twenty-year-olds, and which was presented at a National Symposium on Teenage Sexuality in May of 1991.

Overall statistics from this survey indicated that eighteen per cent of all those surveyed had had sexual intercourse. The older they were, the more common that experience was so that by the age of nineteen, the percentage had gone up to forty-three per cent. Over thirty-five per cent of the whole survey had indulged in heavy petting or the fondling of a friend's genitals, which increased to sixty-four per cent of the nineteen-year-olds in the survey. A total of fifty-four per cent of those attending the church youth clubs surveyed were female and forty-six per cent male. A similar survey conducted in the USA indicated that twenty-four per cent of teenagers in that same age range (thirteen to twenty) had had sexual intercourse. Thirty-one per cent of the teenagers surveyed in the UK from church youth groups felt that it was 'morally acceptable' for two people not married, but both willing, to have sexual intercourse. It is perhaps an indictment upon the church that amongst those surveyed in the UK, thirty-five per cent of them found their prime source of information about sex from their friends, closely followed by thirty-one per cent through sex education at school, but with parents well down the league at only nineteen per cent as a source of information, the Bible at seventeen per cent, and church at an appallingly low seven per cent.

This amount of sexual experimentation does of course have a number of implications. In most teenage sexuality surveys currently being undertaken, considerable concern is expressed by the adolescents about Sexually Transmitted Diseases (STDs). High on any list of STDs is of course AIDS (Acquired Immune Deficiency Syndrome). The national newspapers' survey indicated that girls are more worried about AIDS than boys. However, four in ten teenagers have not changed the way they think about sex and sexual relationships because of the threat of the disease (forty-three per cent of boys and forty-four per cent of girls). In the UK church youth group survey it was some thirty-two per cent who were concerned about AIDS to the extent that this would influence their sexual behaviour. Notwithstanding these relatively high statistics indicating concern over STDs, it was none-the-less true that in 1990 there were 250 million new cases of STDs worldwide. The World Health Organisation estimates that it is the 1,000 million people in the fifteen- to twenty-nine-year-old age group which is most at risk, with up to one in four young people in that age bracket catching a 'minor' STD in 1990, and consequently a considerable possibility of sexually active and infected people transmitting the HIV virus. In the UK, figures for the mid-1980s indicate that at NHS Genito-Urinary Medicine clinics (which deal with ninety per cent of such patients) there were 658,000 new cases of STDs reported and treated.

According to the national newspaper survey, a clear majority were in favour of couples living together before marriage (fifty-six per cent) with only thirteen per cent against setting up home together before the wedding day. It was the seventeen- and eighteen-year-olds who were most in favour of couples living together prior to marriage (fifty-nine per cent). These statistics seem to belie the concern expressed in the same survey about illegitimacy, with forty-six per cent of those questioned feeling that children suffer if their parents are unmarried (fifty-four per cent male believe this compared with thirty-eight per cent female). These attitudes must unfortunately be starkly contrasted with the reality of the results of sexual experimentation in the UK today. The annual number of illegitimate births in England and Wales rose from 48,000 in 1961 to 126,000 in the mid-1980s. Just under eighty per cent of conceptions to women under twenty were illegitimate in the mid-1980s, a percentage which increases to 99.5 per cent of conceptions to girls under sixteen. More than fifty per cent of these conceptions were terminated by abortion during the 1980s, and indeed twenty-five per cent of all abortions in the mid-1980s were carried out on girls under twenty. Less than one per cent of all these abortions were due to a substantial risk of the child being born abnormal.

The prevalence of cohabiting in the UK was more than twice as high amongst women under twenty-five in the mid-1980s as it was for women aged twenty-five to forty-nine. The UK now has approximately 1,000,000 one parent families caring for 1,600,000 children, with one family in eight being headed by a lone parent, and nine out of ten of those parents being women. The indication is that one in five children born today will have divorced parents by the age of sixteen (Family Policies Study Centre, 1986). The sex survey in Christian magazine *Buzz* in 1986 had an encouraging result from the Christian perspective. Forty-five per cent of marriages surveyed indicated that both partners had been virgins on their wedding night, whereas a comparison with non-Christian surveys puts the figure at around eight per cent.

The number of single parent families seems likely to increase as the prevalent trend amongst surveyed teenagers in the UK indicates that the better option to an unhappy marriage is, for them, either abortion (hence the increase in the number of abortions) or the viability of an illegitimate child. So, out of the 119,000 teenage pregnancies in 1985, where eighty-four per cent of them were outside marriage, a third of the girls chose to have an abortion (ten years earlier only twenty-five per cent had done so), whilst those marrying the father dropped from twenty-one per cent in 1975 to eleven per cent in 1985. Social Trends 1990, looking at abortion statistics around Europe and quoted by Interpol, revealed the following horrifying comparisons: the chances of being killed by terrorists are 1 in 42,000; the chances of being killed by homicide in Norway are 1 in 100,000; yet the chances of being killed in the womb of a British woman are 1 in 5.3. Social deprivation and the governmentally godless society (ie, atheistic systems, such as communism) have rendered the much reported situation in Romania even worse, where the chances of being killed in the womb of a Romanian woman are now 1 in 1.6. These are some of the disturbing trends, and horrifying consequences, of much sexual experimentation most usually begun during adolescence.

Of course, much sexual experimentation amongst adolescents starts with auto-eroticism or masturbation. It has been estimated that during the period of adolescence, ninety per cent of males masturbate with some frequency, or in the words of the old adage, 'Nine out of ten lads do, and the tenth is a liar!' The percentage for females is considerably lower, at forty per cent, which has more to do with external genitalia, and sexual stimulation trigger points in the male, than it has to do with heightened sexuality. It is my opinion that any parent, teacher or church youth leader working with young people will have to be open, honest and frank in his or her discussion of this subject. It has for years remained a taboo subject, producing endless generations of guilt-ridden individuals who are unclear in their own mind and conscience concerning the morality (or even physical dangers!) of such a common practice. It needs to be said very clearly that the Bible is providentially silent on the subject, not because I think God does not want the subject discussed, but because it is not the big issue that many Christian leaders have hypocritically made it out to be. We cannot, in our dealings with adolescents, cater our morality to the lowest common denominator of our own past failures, but neither can we impose upon adolescents strictures and disciplines which are unbiblical and unworkable. And ones which we ourselves never kept to!

No amount of twisting faulty exegesis around Genesis 38:9 can make Scripture speak on this subject. That passage has more to do with methods and motives of conception and contraception within a cultural setting, than it has to do with masturbation, despite having loaned to auto-eroticism the name of 'Onanism'. We would do better as with all our biblical exegesis to understand the whole tenor of Scripture and the character of God as revealed by the Holy Spirit and in Jesus, rather than seek to establish criteria through proof texts. A proof text out of context is a pretext!

When it comes to the area of masturbation, a practice which starts most usually during puberty and particularly amongst males, it seems to me that in the face of the Bible's silence on the subject, a good place to start is with the proposition that, ' ''Everything is permissible'' – but not everything is beneficial. ''Everything is permissible'' – but not everything is constructive' (1 Cor 10:23). If we are to maintain biblical integrity and godly morality, as we surely must – by our lifestyle, our demonstration, our explanation and our words – towards adolescents, then in denying them sexual intercourse outside of marriage, as the Bible clearly teaches, it seems to me we must be all the more careful before we make unbiblical demands of those same adolescents concerning the exercise of their sexual drive, at its peak at the age of eighteen, through the controlled use of masturbation. My own position is that I would never advocate masturbation, but nor will I forbid it. From personal experience and from that of those whom I have had the privilege of counselling, it seems to me that to masturbate is physically and emotionally normal, and not to masturbate is also physically and emotionally normal.

It does seem, however, that there are three potential areas where problems arise. The first is the area of condemnation, which is not unlinked to the intense feelings of elation immediately prior to masturbation, followed by the sensation of depression consequent to orgasm and, in the male's case, ejaculation. This is a prime time for the Enemy to condemn the individual over his or her sexuality, attraction to members of the opposite sex, hormonal drive, and particularly to condemn in the area of his or her relationship to God, which Satan would maintain is impaired through masturbation. Consequently, I have had to speak to countless numbers of young lads who have seen the whole area of auto-eroticism as *the* major problem in their walk with God. In *every case* I have found other areas of their lifestyle to be of much greater concern from God's perspective, according to Scripture and the witness of the Holy Spirit. So, God will be more at pains to point out the nature of the relationship between the teenager and his parents, or his brother or sister, or his dishonesty, or his aggression, rather than the area of masturbation. The condemnation which sweeps in after the act of auto-eroticism is usually clearly identifiable as being from the Enemy because:

a) all condemnation comes from him (Rom 8:1), and

b) the condemnation is usually of a general nature and

runs along the lines of: 'You're no good; you've failed yet again; you could never be a good Christian; you'll never make the grade', and consequently

c) does not carry with it specific conviction and the motivation and ability to stop and change. When the Holy Spirit convicts, as opposed to the Enemy condemning, such conviction is always clear, specific, and facilitates repentance and change. When it comes to masturbation, in the vast majority of cases, it is not conviction of the Holy Spirit which is at work but condemnation of the Enemy.

The second problem area connected to this matter is that of the need for comfort. It is true that a number of young people get locked into a cycle of masturbation because of their inherent insecurities and need for self-comfort. This cycle of behaviour can be triggered by loneliness, rejection, emotional trauma, strong sensations of inadequacy, and insecurities ranging from self-worth through to sexual orientation. The tendency then is that the adolescent is driven to comfort himself by indulging in auto-eroticism. Under such circumstances masturbation is clearly unhelpful. It is not insignificant that under such circumstances, when love and security, self-worth and belonging are poured into the adolescent's life, the frequency of masturbation decreases, not increases – an observation which can also be made when such an adolescent finds a girlfriend. One would think that when this happens the frequency of masturbation would go up, but in fact it often goes down. In these circumstances masturbation is clearly not a root problem, but rather a symptom of a deeper root problem, and the issues must be dealt with at that root level.

The third area where masturbation becomes a problem is confusion of roles. From a biblical and Christian viewpoint, the giving of one's body in intimate sexual knowledge (the Old Testament concept of 'knowing' God uses the same idea of sexual intimacy as when a man 'knows' or has intercourse with a woman) is to be preserved for the context of marriage, and is about giving rather than receiving. In marriage the ideal of sexual fulfilment is that the husband gives himself away fully to the wife whilst looking out for her needs and desires – emotional, social, relational and physical – whilst she does the same for her husband. To this extent, sex and sexuality is about giving, not receiving. However, when it comes to auto-eroticism, as the very word itself indicates, there is a confusion of roles. The role of giver is combined with the role of receiver. Thus the adolescent who indulges in masturbation is all too quickly subsumed by a selfish obsession which, in seeking for external outlets, will often focus itself upon the fantasy life. This can in turn lead to problems with pornographic literature and video tapes, and promote an unhealthy sex life in the mind which will certainly be detrimental to real-life sex later on in the marriage bed! For some even, the fantasy becomes preferable to later reality. Any masturbation which deliberately focuses its target mentally upon specific individuals is clearly wrong, unhelpful and a violation of the Matthew 5:27–30 principle, where Jesus speaks more about motivation behind thinking rather than the initial thought, since there is clearly a difference between initial temptation and subsequent sin (Heb 4:15).

When dealing with the lives of young adolescents on the subject of masturbation, be aware that any one of these three potential problem areas (condemnation, comfort, confusion of roles) can lead to an out-of-control habit pattern which in and of itself is also wrong, since the Bible clearly teaches that we should be the masters of our bodies and not they the masters of us. My counsel, when it comes to the subject of masturbation, would always therefore be: 'You should be free to masturbate, and you should be free not to masturbate. You should be able to. You should be able to stop.' This is an ideal towards which I will work in the area of physical change and sexuality in the lives of adolescents.

If the Bible is providentially silent on the subject of masturbation, we must, as parents, youth workers and youth leaders, be equally clear as to what the Bible says when it comes to the area of sex outside marriage. And not only what it says but why it says it. It is important that we do not deny adolescents the valid parameters within which they are experimenting, to find out who they are and what they can and cannot do. We must also remember that such parameters must be reasonable and explained, for such is the nature of our God and his Book. Thus when it comes to teenage sexual promiscuity we must understand that God is a sexual being, in so much that he had the first sexual thought and created male and female, both in his image, as sexual beings. Sex in the first place was God's idea (Gen 1:28–31). God clearly and repeatedly says that sexual intercourse outside of marriage is wrong. References you might find helpful follow, because I have met a number of adolescents *and* youth leaders who, whilst believing generally that the Bible teaches that sex outside marriage is wrong, can neither say where it says so or why it says it.

Look at the following references: 1 Cor 6:18, Mt 15:19, Jn 8:41, Rom 13:13, 1 Cor 7:9, Gal 5:19, Eph 5:1, Col 3:5, 1 Thess 4:3, 2 Tim 2:22 and Rev 21:8.

The biblical reasons behind chastity before marriage are quite simple. Firstly, it is a command of God, which would have to be the criterion if Jesus Christ is the boss of the individual adolescent. Secondly, because of the extremely high levels of commitment which such intimacy demands, God has placed the outworking of such a commitment as a lifelong monogamy. This is the only framework within which such commitment can be experimented with and be expected to grow in a safe environment. Many people suffer from sexual malfunction in marriage because of former adolescent sexual experimentation outside of it, with all the guilt which that entails.

Thirdly, the Bible clearly teaches that the essential

content of sexual intercourse is not merely physical, emotional and relational, but also spiritual. The apostle Paul uses an analogy linking the husband and wife to Christ and the church, and maintains that there is a deep mystery involved in the husband and wife becoming one flesh (Eph 5:31–32). Now, any spiritual union can only take place in one of two kingdoms: it will either be in Satan's or in God's. And if God has commanded that sexual intercourse should not take place outside of marriage (and he has!) then such spiritual union as occurs when sexual intercourse happens outside of marriage must be in Satan's kingdom. This is not theory but rather has its practical results. I have had to pray with and counsel a number of couples or male individuals where it appears that through sex outside of marriage, sexual oppression and demonic activity has been passed on by one partner to the other.

Fourthly, there is a creation principle involved in sexual intercourse in that whilst it is not solely for the purpose of procreation, this is one of its main functions. The impregnation, conception, gestation and lactation of children is, in Scripture, all a part of family life, where each family derives its name from God, the father of all families and the original father (Father, Son and Holy Spirit – Eph 3:14–15). Endeavours to denigrate family life (by which I do not solely mean the nuclear family, a western concept) have proven socially, economically, and emotionally destructive around Eastern Europe since the turn of the century and the advent of communism. However, western society has shown the equally destructive power of procreation out of the context of the stable family environment and lifelong commitment between two partners, as advocated by God and his book (see earlier statistics on abortion and illegitimacy).

The fifth reason for restricting sexual intercourse within the confines of marriage is the whole realm of care. We have already looked at the horrifying statistics on the rise of STDs, and it remains true to say that heterosexual monogamous fidelity remains the only (and God's) solution to such widespread incidence. This is now the officially stated position on AIDS by the World Health Organisation. Sexual promiscuity and experimentation amongst adolescents does account for an increase in cervical cancer amongst teenage girls. Early introduction of the pill to those who are sexually active from an early age, can promote an increase in such detrimental side effects as high blood pressure, thrombosis, weight gain and hormonal imbalance.

Like attracts like?

An area which we touched on briefly when we looked at the different age ranges into which adolescence falls, was the so-called 'homosexual phase', a phase which is both common and normal, though *not* natural. In using the word natural, I am referring to biblical creation principles whereby before the Fall, male and female were created to relate together sexually in the context of marriage, and not male to male or female to female (homosexual meaning like sex to like sex). It is true that in a fallen and an unredeemed state it might 'feel' entirely 'natural' for a male to want to have sex with another male, or at least to experiment in that area during adolescence, but those 'natural' feelings are then being measured by some kind of internal and entirely subjective emotive response rather than the external absolute of God's character, his creation and his word.

Surveys conducted in the United States by Masters and Johnson during the 1950s and again in the 1970s indicated that one in twenty-five people were exclusively homosexual in orientation, which is to say that they never remember having feelings or sexual attraction for members of the opposite sex. However, those same surveys indicated that up to three in ten had had homosexual experiences, with the majority of those happening during the years of adolescence.

Whilst there is no evidence that homosexuality is the result of a chemical or hormonal genetic imbalance, there is a considerable amount of evidence to indicate that it can be the result of very early environmental emphases. Thus homes with an absent father or an overly dominant mother *may* have considerable impact on the sexual orientation of any male children brought up in that environment. Such behaviour is learned, albeit often on a subconscious level, and occurs during the formative years (two to six), and also more consciously and with wilful decisions taken during adolescence (ten to twenty-one). The latter is because adolescence is a time for questioning the role and self-worth of the adolescent and how he or she relates to those around them, and a time when role models are extremely important. The lack of physical and emotional affection properly expressed by a father to a son will result in a serious loss of role model for that young male adolescent. An uncaring, remote or even removed mother can seriously damage the sexual and emotional development of an adolescent daughter. These are generalities, but there is evidence to indicate that they frequently hold true. The result is that the young person validly searches for love, affection and approval from someone of their own sex, but without the correct role model will often correlate such love and approval on the sexual level because of all that is happening within them due to physical change in adolescence. This can lead to homosexual experimentation, and later orientation.

There is some evidence to suggest that single sex environments (eg, boarding schools and remand homes) can have a similar effect upon the sexual orientation of the developing adolescent. It is also true that sometimes a strict religious upbringing, where the possibility of sexual relationships with members of the *opposite* sex are so legalistically and severely clamped down upon, can produce a strange backlash in the mentality of the individual adolescent, whereby, if heterosexual contact is forbidden, homosexual contact must be okay! In such circumstances, homosexual experimentation becomes another form of relief of sexual tension, much akin to masturbation. This is one explanation why so-called 'horse play' and much physical contact often goes on amongst young adolescent males. This not infrequently (up to thirty per cent) results in homosexual experimentation, often in the form of mutual masturbation.

It is precisely because adolescence is such a time of emotional turmoil, experimentation, uncertainty and insecurity, that young people are particularly vulnerable, including in the area of their sexual orientation. That is why there are inherent dangers in claims that Harringay Council in London would prosecute parents who kept their children away from lessons on homosexuality, claims which were to be investigated in an enquiry launched by the then Education Secretary, Kenneth Baker. It is why there are dangers in the gay recruitment drive in Brent London Council which resulted in an enormous response amongst homosexuals toward the challenge of taking influential school governorships in local primary and secondary schools. Ex-Education Director, Adrian Parsons left his £30,000 a year post with that council because he could no longer tolerate political interference and objected to Brent's policy of positive discrimination with regard to sexual orientation when it came to filling key posts. Pertinent to all these situations is the fact that homosexual experimentation remains normal, though not natural. That experimentation is not the same thing as fixed orientation.

It is also important to understand what the Bible teaches on homosexuality. Like any sin, the sinner is loved of God and a candidate for his forgiveness, grace and mercy. But the practice of homosexuality itself is comprehensively condemned with reasoned explanations given (Rom 1:21–32, 1 Cor 6:8–11, 18, 1 Tim 1:9, Lev 18:22, Lev 20:9, 13, Gen 19:1–10, Judg 19:22, Ezek 16:48–49). Biblically, homosexual practice is forbidden because sexual union is reserved only for marriage, and marriage is reserved only for male and female. Homosexuality also contravenes the created order physically, emotionally and socially, and it denies the *duality* of the Godhead (Gen 1:27, Rom 8:15, Is 66:12–14, Mt 23:37 – references which indicate both the father and mother heart of God).

We need to look at one other implication for sexuality which physical change brings about in the lives of adolescents. This is the whole subject of what the Bible calls 'unequal yoking'.

If much physical change begins at puberty, and puberty produces much sexual stimulus in thought, and potentially in experimentation; if the physical peak is reached at seventeen (hence the increasing number of young athletes you will see on your TV screen) and the male sexual peak is reached at eighteen – then we must be aware of the implications of male to female attraction when it comes to the planning of our youth group, or the social rules we make for dating for our own offspring! The facts are simple: by and large, young adolescents will want by the age of sixteen or so to be developing more exclusive relationships with members of the opposite sex (see the age bands in the previous chapter). The Bible is clear that Christians should aim to go out with (and eventually marry, if that is appropriate) members of the opposite sex who are as committed to God as they are. The principle is obvious – if you are standing on a table trying to pull someone up to be with you, it is much more likely that they will pull you down to be with them! We have all heard of, and may know personal examples of, Christians who have gone out with non-Christians and subsequently those people have been converted. These however, are exceptions to the rule. These are evidences of God's grace, not indications of his methodology! It is impossible to share anything of oneself on an emotional, mental, social and ultimately (within marriage) physical level beyond the merely superficial with someone who does not hold the same world philosophy as yourself, and even more importantly, with someone who does not have a living relationship with God in the same way that you do. That is true of all ages, and not just adolescents, but the temptation is particularly strong during adolescence when all these physical and sexual changes are taking place.

I would want to argue that the Bible's teaching on 'unequal yoking' (1 Cor 15:33, 2 Cor 6:14) applies not only from the believer's to the unbeliever's perspective, but also from the committed to the less committed. This does mean that when you take into account physical change and development in the lives of the adolescents closest to you, it must have practical implications on the way you plan your youth group programme, or the parameters that you set for social interaction and dating for your own children. A simple rule is that you make provision for your hopefully committed Christian adolescents to meet other equally committed Christian adolescents of the opposite sex! If your youth group is heavily weighted in one direction concerning gender, then it is incumbent upon you to make sure that you book social times with another church youth group where the reverse is true! Welcoming your son's latest girlfriend into the family household with reasoned, but adhered to, parameters of behaviour is far more productive than expressing an unreasonable and instinctive dislike of her. Over-protective fathers and coddling mothers are distinctly unhelpful when it comes to the subject of unequal yoking!

Obviously, we have had to major in this chapter on the sexual connotations of physical development in the life of an adolescent. There are, however, a number of minor pointers that are worth remembering when it comes to helping us understand the physical changes of adolescents. The first relates to hygiene.

In the survey done around church youth groups, when asked to rate themselves according to the three categories – kind, intelligent and popular – the average score indicated that the adolescents involved were seventy-five per cent *dissatisfied* with their self-image. There is an obvious physical extension of this dissatisfaction with self-image which embraces appearance, fashion, strength, athleticism, weight and body shape, and dissatisfaction with external genitalia. This increase in physical awareness is usually marked in pubescent adolescents by an increased awareness of bodily hygiene. Up until adolescence, there are to most young people two dirty words: one is soap; the other is water; and when combined they seem to be lethal! However, with the onset of puberty, personal hygiene suddenly becomes an important and time-consuming matter. Males discover under-arm deodorant, aftershave and talcum powder. Females discover the same (perfume rather than aftershave!) and have an increased access to make-up. The guys begin shaving and all too quickly betray the bloody evidence. And both sexes become increasingly aware of and susceptible to spots, or in the worst-case scenario, the dreaded acne! Where once it seemed impossible to get your son or daughter *into* the bathroom on a school morning, now it seems impossible to get them out! In many cases cleanliness seems to usurp godliness, and physical appearance becomes all-important. Pocket money will be lavished on make-up, skin care, toiletries, aftershaves and hair preparations. An increased awareness of hygiene due to an increase of body odours is one root of symptoms. The other is the desire to be socially and physically acceptable, particularly amongst peer groups, whilst emulating adults. Thus, adolescent males will often adorn themselves with aftershave before they even begin shaving.

Another area related to physical change that is worth mentioning is the purely physical reason behind some of the marked mood swings observable in adolescents, particularly in females. This has much to do with the release and occasional imbalance of chemical hormones within the body, and certainly where females are concerned, will be most markedly apparent at that time of the month. Most adolescent girls will understand this of their peers; most adolescent boys will not have a clue. It is incumbent upon teachers, youth leaders and parents to understand this and to be unembarrassed by it. So some mood swings will be chemically induced and have more to do with physical change than with emotional change.

A final mention concerning physical change and development must go to the whole area of clumsiness. As I grew up through adolescence, I gained something of a reputation for extreme clumsiness. If there was something to be dropped, I would drop it. If there was something to be knocked over, I would knock it over. If there was anything to be smashed, Pete would be the one to smash it! So much so that I actually acquired the nickname 'bullethead'. This didn't so much say something about the physical shape and development of my head, as about my proclivity towards tripping over objects on the floor and banging my head against the wall – a fact which my friends often think provides an explanation for much of my current behaviour! (My daughter Freddi seems now to have inherited the same proclivity!)

The fact of the matter is that I suffered agonies of embarrassment and not a few accusations of carelessness throughout my adolescent years because of my clumsiness. And I have subsequently met many young people who suffer the same. I have even had to pray with some adults who have been haunted by the curse of negative words spoken over them in their adolescence because of their apparent clumsiness.

Such adolescent tendency towards clumsiness deserves an explanation. We have already seen that puberty within adolescence marks the most exaggerated growth spurt in the life of an individual. This growth is so extreme (ask any parent who has had to buy his or her child new shoes or new trousers all too regularly!) that there are occasions when misinformation is fed between brain and body extremities. Picture the scene! Aunt Mary has arrived for afternoon tea. Young Peter is asked to pass the cup and saucer to his aunt. Peter's brain tells him that Peter's arm is twenty-four inches long and accordingly orders the reflex nerve ending and muscle responses to stretch for a cup and saucer at a twenty-four inch distance. In actual fact, Peter's brain has fed him misinformation since it has not yet registered the fact that Peter's arm is now twenty-four-and-a-half inches long due to the adolescent growth spurt! Result: one knocked-over cup of tea into the lap of Aunt Mary!

It is a fact of life that the brain does not always keep in pace with the physical development of the adolescent. This also partially explains why some adolescents are unco-ordinated and ungainly in their movements. It also explains embarrassment linked to physical activities in early puberty (as opposed to later puberty when the body is honing itself to its physical peak), and therefore the reluctance of some young adolescents to take part in sports, drama or dancing activities. Obviously there are social embarrassment factors involved here too, but the physical ones should not be underestimated.

Well, there we have it! A quick overview of the main areas of physical change and development in the life of an adolescent. If that seems a lot and too much to cope with, just remember that that's only one of the five main life areas which are changing in an interrelated fashion, all at the same time! In the next chapter we will go on to look at how you and I can better understand the emotional development of the adolescent.

CHAPTER SEVEN

MORE THAN FEELINGS?

– THE EMOTIONAL DEVELOPMENT OF THE ADOLESCENT

Fears will be more frightening . . . Pleasures will be more exciting . . . Irritations will be more distressing, and . . . Frustrations will be more intolerable. Every experience will appear kingsized. Emotions move quickly up and down . . . They are . . . human yo-yo's.

From James Dobson, *Preparing For Adolescence* (Kingsway Publications: Eastbourne, 1982).

Adolescence often seems to be characterised by a bundle of sometimes raw emotions combined with a package of vibrant energy, wrapped up in a changing body. Understanding and coming to terms with the emotional development of an adolescent will necessitate the focus of our attention around two key words: the first is intensity; the second is inconsistency.

Intensity

It is inadequate and unreal to write off the emotions of the developing adolescent as being the results of mere whim or fantasy. Adolescent emotions may lack the grounding of experience and mature reflection that occasionally adulthood will bring, but they are none the less very real. Oftentimes the adolescent is experiencing emotions previously dormant (as with awakening sexual awareness), and the power or intensity of those emotions takes the adolescent by surprise. Sometimes, however, the adolescent, because the emotion is new to him or her, tends to push the experience of the emotion as far as possible – and to the observing adult there then seem to be no reasonable bounds or limits to the intensity of that emotion. And so rage, joy or romantic infatuation can seem to be running at levels disproportionate to their causes. Often, because the adolescent is undergoing an emotion not based on any previous experience, there will again be a lack of perspective in the spectrum of the adolescent's emotions. thus, good feelings will tend never to have felt so good, and the expectation will be that they can never be bettered. Equally, bad feelings will always be the worst possible, and these pendulum extremes will often send the adolescent into 'emotional swings.'

The intensity of adolescent emotions means that adolescence is a time when great attachments are formed to people or to projects. Emotionally, adolescence is the age of causes. These causes may vary as widely as support for ecological projects, a local football team, a film or pop star or even for the local church youth group! The converse is also true, whereby adolescents can form emotional antipathies towards people and projects. No one is ever loved so passionately nor hated so vitriolically as by an adolescent.

The implications of the dominance of emotions in adolescence are very clear in our churches. In Great Britain, fifty-six per cent of church leavers leave because their church life is dominated by a sense of loneliness and a lack of emotionally satisfying peer relationships (same age and background). The average age of those leavers is twenty-one years. The importance of emotional attachment and the need for heroes and role models is so great during adolescence that the lack of it means that adolescents are voting with their feet when it comes to church attendance.

Heroes

The posters, videos, CDs and tapes that populate the walls and shelves of many an adolescent's bedroom also bear witness to the emotional intensity and need for heroes and role models. A recent national newspaper survey, polling more than 1,000 teenagers in 1990, determined the nature of some of the adolescents' heroes and role models, with Frank Bruno coming out on top in the sports realm with thirty-four per cent, Eddie Murphy in the film world with twenty-one per cent, the rock band U2 with a result of eleven per cent, Nelson Mandela topping the politicians' arena at thirty-four per cent, and Lenny Henry coming first in the area of TV stardom and personalities with a comfortable twenty-four per cent. Emotional attachment to such figures should not be underestimated, and is a projection by adolescents of a need to identify with something other than and outside of themselves, with attributes of fame, wealth, success, intelligence and idealism, often not felt by the adolescent, but apparently observed in the life and lifestyle of his or her hero.

It needs also to be understood that these emotional attachments and the search for a hero or role model does not only occur in the world of music, entertainment and politics, but also strikes nearer to home, taking the form of the adolescent 'crush'. It has been noted in Chapter 6 that this emotional crush often starts with the same sex but usually moves on to opposite sex attraction. The adolescent crush has sometimes been called 'puppy love', which is an extremely unhelpful and patronising term, particularly as it carries the implication that the feelings are not real. The feelings involved in young love may well not be rooted in experience and might originally derive from a romantic notion of love where basically the adolescent is in love with being in love. However, the emotions involved are both real and intense. There are certainly lessons to be learned here for the unsuspecting teacher, youth leader, or youth counsellor. The basic ground rules for Christian propriety and wisdom must therefore remain true for the adolescent as for the adult: males deal with/counsel/pray for males, and females for females. Even then, exclusive one-to-one 'lock-up' must be avoided.

It is true that adolescents often revel in emotional experience, enjoying the emotions for their own sake, and pushing them to extremes of both pain and pleasure, a little like testing the site of a previous toothache with your tongue, to either enjoy the absence of pain or affirm its continuation! Because adolescent emotions are so near to the surface, are so keenly felt and often so greatly enjoyed (or at least experimented with), our youth activities, programmes, discipleship, evangelism, and parenting must all seek to make an emotional engagement in the life of the adolescent concerned. The reason why sixty-three per cent of church leavers left their church was because they were thoroughly bored (lack of emotional engagement) with the format of their church service, particularly in the area of worship, and the average age of those church leavers was only twenty.

Introspection

Another hallmark of the intensity of the emotional development of adolescents is their proclivity towards self-examination. This often takes the form of endless conversations about themselves, their background, their actions and reactions, how they feel and how they have felt. These emotional self-examinations are attempts by the adolescents to identify their true feelings and personalities by reflecting them through other people (in later adolescence the one-to-one pairing, in middle adolescence the small clique, and in early adolescence the gang mentality). Sometimes the people required to listen to these emotional self-examinations will not be peers, but instead be adults (teachers, youth workers, parents). It is often observable that when the adolescent is bearing his or her emotions within a peer group context, the interreaction is to gain access and acceptance to the group, usually through attempts to impress them. Alternately, when the adolescent is firing emotionally in an adult context, the interreaction is often designed to shock or in some way rebel against the adult's conception of that adolescent. This is certainly not always the case, but either method of emotional exposure is valid in terms of development. The greater danger is when adolescents bottle up their emotions, finding neither positive nor negative expression for them with their peer groups or surrounding adults.

Suicide

Unfortunately, intensity of emotions does lead to prevalence of teenage suicides. There are many sociological factors involved in the massive increase in teenage suicide observed by the Samaritans. Suicide now accounts for thirty per cent of all teenage deaths. These must of course include a general sense of angst derived from the continuing threat of destabilised world politics and the possibility of nuclear holocaust. Fear of sexually transmitted disease, and the involvement in drug abuse with its inherent potential for passing on disease, are also significant contributing factors to teenage suicide. Unemployment, with its devastating effect upon self-worth and its apparent denial of destiny and the damning implications of materialistic failure in a materialistic society are also in the mix, as is concern over long-term damage to the environment.

However, underlying all of these specific reasons is a more disturbing trend identified clearly by sociologist Emile

Durkheim, who links the rise in teenage suicide to emotional trauma caused by the condition of anomie. Anomie is a condition caused by a lack of external and clearly defined social norms leading to lassitude and depression. In searching for personal worth and identity, with assessment of one's role within peer groups (gangs, cliques and then one-to-one relationships), plus intensity of mood swings and a testing of parameters of acceptable behaviour, married as we will see in Chapter 7 to a degree of intellectual experimentation, there is produced a combination which makes insecurity one of the key words for adolescent development. We have seen in Chapter 4 that society in general has, through a progression of historical reactions, reached a place where morally, legally and relationally the parameters and guidelines have been decried and often negated. This has not helped adolescent insecurity. As the post-war restrictions of the last half of the forties gave way to the more hopeful optimism of the fifties, and then the psychedelic hedonism of the liberal sixties, so the materialism of the seventies ushered in the god of technology which in its apparent barrenness gave way to the search for spiritual truth embodied in the gurus of the eighties. We have emerged now in the nineties with a society bereft of the values of community, neighbourliness, distrustful of government and legal systems, acutely aware of the bankruptcy of the purely technological and material, yet failing to adopt the investment of past generations in any kind of orthodox or organised religious or moral codes of behaviour. Rather, society has indulged in an orgy of individualistic libertarian experimentations with thoughts, morality, legalities and spirituality (hence the increase of the dawn of the New Age), and in this plethora of experimentation it is not only unhelpful *barriers* which have been knocked down, but positive and useful *boundaries* which have been swept away. Adolescents thus find themselves in a sea of uncertainty. What is expected of them is no longer clear.

The social norms that once defined adulthood have been themselves removed. Adolescents suddenly realise that not only are they in a state of transition, but they are not even sure what it is that they are moving towards! Such a lack of definition and expectation causes a high level of anxiety (anomie) and provides us with a useful pointer in helping us understand the emotional development of adolescents – and it goes some way to explaining the prevalence of adolescent suicide.

Helpful boundaries

Emotional development, like any other form of development, does require stated, recognised, explained and reasonable parameters. Even whilst experiencing a turmoil of swinging emotions, adolescents need to be encouraged to understand that adults choose to live not from emotions, but from moral decisions of the will. Every emotion is preceded by a thought. Adolescents also need to be encouraged to realise why their emotions swing in the way they do. And they need to be persuaded to take moral responsibility for the outworking of those emotions in terms of their behaviour towards themselves, their family, their peers, in the spheres of their education, their recreation and their occupation. It is a part of the healthy emotional development of adolescents that they are not left with too much freedom and with too many decisions to make as they develop. If they are, bewilderment, turpitude, depression and possibly ultimately suicide may result. A number of parents who have faced the tragic loss of their adolescent children through suicide have expressed great surprise as they were completely unaware of the emotional state of their child, thinking them to be generally happy and well-balanced. It needs to be remembered that whenever adolescents bottle up these feelings, or simply fail to understand them, there remains the possibility of this kind of tragic outcome.

Unhelpful barriers

It also needs to be remembered that in the emotional development of adolescents the reverse is true. If adolescent suicide can be caused by the lack of defined social norms, referred to above as anomie, it can also be caused by the placing of too many restrictions and too tight a system of regulations around the life of the developing youngster. Asking adolescents to self-regulate their development, to make too many decisions, and to give them too much freedom is one cause of the emotional turmoil which can lead to suicide. But taking from adolescents all rights of self-determination and the responsibility for any decision-making process, enforcing restrictions with too little freedom and unreasonable, unexplained parameters can just as readily throw adolescents into a state of depression leading to suicide. The balance is not an easy one to achieve, but God's understanding of the transition periods of adolescence, his inbuilt strengths into every stage of growth in the individual (see Chapter 3) and his grace and wisdom available to those who ask for it (Jas 1:5) can help us on the way to achieving such a balance. It is generally true that the adolescent feels that he needs *more* room to develop than he actually does, whilst the responsible adult tends to think he needs *less* room than he actually does. The balance is therefore to be achieved by compromise on both sides, with give and take from both the adult and the adolescent.

'Put away childish things'

There is one common adolescent emotion which appears remarkable for its lack of intensity, and which occurs within many adolescents. This is the emotion (or non-emotion?) of boredom, or apparent boredom. The despairing parent, or youth leader, will be all too familiar with the scenario where after hours of thought and preparation and the expenditure of high levels of energy in order to provide an exhilarating and exciting experience (a weekend away, a game of baseball, a pro-active Bible study, a rock concert, a session of manic praise and worship, an evening's youth group activities, and so on), the response on the part of the adolescent is: 'that was boring.' Or when asked if the activity was enjoyed, replies: 'It was all right.' Even as I write the words, the experienced youth worker will be able to hear the inflection in the adolescent's voice: a falling inflection, tailing away as the adolescent walks off into the middle distance!

Unless we understand the emotional projectionism which is going on here, such a reaction can produce despair or intensely irritate the average youth leader/youth worker/parent. The reaction has simple roots (though seldom as defined and realised as follows), operating usually at a subconscious level. The problem for the adolescent is that emotional enthusiasm is indissolubly linked in their mind, memory and experience to their state as a child. Excited enthusiasm and totally absorbing commitment is something which adolescents tend to associate with a state of childhood from which they are trying to escape. They are no longer children. If children get excited, they will not. If children express enthusiasm they will not. If children give ready feedback in order to win the approval or attention of adults, they will not. If children in their enthusiastic response demonstrate a certain dependency upon adults for their enjoyment and activities, they will not.

Enthusiasm is one of the attributes which God wants us to recapture, having gone through this understandable phase of adolescence, if we are to see and inherit the kingdom of God as do little children. It is perhaps not insignificant that the word enthusiasm comes from two Greek words, *en theos* – which mean 'of God'. Adolescents are, of course, capable of enormous enthusiasm. But it is true that usually an outward veneer of boredom, passivity and apathy has to be broken through before such enthusiasm can be released and harnessed. Emotional involvement in a youth programme, or a church worship or teaching meeting can be obtained from ten- to fourteen-year olds through the use of concrete examples, visual aids, stories and jokes, dramas and role plays, visual aids and audio-visual aids.

Around the fourteen to fifteen mark and upwards, emotional investment can be gained by exactly the same techniques, but this time the adolescent will, at least initially, assume the appearance of indifference. Those in Year 10 at school are as emotionally captivated by the personal testimony of a visiting Christian speaker as those in Year 9, but the difference is that Year 10 will pretend not to be! Methods of breaking through the veneer (for example, disarming the reactions of Year 10 by highlighting them before going into the personal testimony) will need to be added on in order to break through this veneer of apparent boredom. Passivity and apathy, which are often associated with a bored reaction, can come from either the same root of not wishing to be seen to be enthusiastic, or can be due to adolescents being precipitated into inactivity because of their uncertainty as to which direction to take (anomie again). Or because of their rebellion against the direction imposed upon them by an external authority (youth leader, parent, teacher, or the youth programme itself).

Having identified intensity as one of the two key hallmarks of adolescent emotional development, let's move on to examine the second.

Inconsistency

Ask any youth leader what he or she doesn't like about the average adolescent and one of the answers that will crop up is their unpredictability – the inconsistency of their emotions. One moment they seem to be fine; the next they are in deep pits of despair. One moment they seem to be friendly; the next they're evincing all the symptoms of the proverbial 'cold shoulder'. One reason for this inconsistency is precisely because the emotions felt by the adolescent tend to be so extreme in their intensity, as we have already seen. However, it is impossible to maintain such intensity of emotion for too long and consequently a peak of adolescent emotion (be it positive or negative) will tend almost inevitably to be followed by a trough of opposing emotions. These peaks and troughs can go in cycles which are as rapid as mere minutes, or as extended as several days. Thus an inconsistent mood swing may manifest itself several times over the course of an evening's youth group, whilst an adolescent 'crush' may last for several weeks, and a teenage hero may find favour for up to a year-and-a-half. Since any youth generation is approximately two years long only (ie, those in Years 7 and 8 at school will mingle, but those from Years 7 and 9 will not), it can be wearying for the adult to attempt to keep up with such inconsistencies. There is, however, a positive aspect to these inconsistencies. The peaks and troughs of emotions tend to act as a kind of safety valve in the development of adolescents, giving much needed time off from the rack of over-stretched feelings.

As adolescents also seek to determine how they are perceived by the world of the adult, and as they endeavour to discover what the acceptable parameters of feelings and behaviour are, another cause of emotional inconsistency emerges. Adolescents deliberately test the reactions of the adult. A suitable analogy would be the flexing of emotional muscles. Adolescents are seeking to provoke reaction from the adult world, by pushing first in one direction as hard as possible and following up immediately with a push in the opposite direction. The result is that the adolescent is kept emotionally off balance, testing the boundaries of acceptable behaviour and determining what the *real* feelings of the adult are towards the adolescent. The reasoning (and *sometimes* this is deliberate) goes something like this: 'If I display this emotional behaviour here, you react favourably. How will you react if I display these emotional reactions over here?' It is a kind of emotional probing to determine the acceptance and commitment levels of the adult towards the adolescent. Inconsistent emotions can also be the hallmark of the adolescent struggle against authority and against the 'pack' mentality, even though peer group pressure and the need to belong will also cause opposite (and therefore inconsistent) emotions to come into play. The adolescent is pro the 'gang', and at the same time is struggling for individual, independent recognition. Inconsistency indeed!

Of course, emotional development cannot be segregated from other aspects of adolescent development in a real world, and it is true that emotional inconsistency can also be attributed to hormonal imbalance in the lives of both male and female adolescents, though this is most particularly marked in the massive release of hormones on the monthly menstrual cycle. This, in its early days of getting established in the life of the female adolescent, can be particularly extreme, and can provoke the most obvious of emotional reactions and inconsistencies. Similarly, with the increase of physical development and sexual awareness, triggered by puberty, there comes an emotional reaction best described as flirtation. Adolescents, in attempting to test the extent of their attractiveness to (mainly) members of the other sex, can on occasions flirt outrageously, only to later drop the object of their apparent infatuation. Flirtation, with all of its ritual of sexual signals and emotional advances, tends by its very nature to be short-lived and inconsistent.

Discovering identity

Finally, as we seek to understand the emotional development of adolescents, we must bear in mind that these are years reserved for the discovery of individual identity. Coming to the emotional fore in the lives of many adolescents is the tumult of intense personal likes and dislikes, directed not only at people and things around them, but also internalised and directed at themselves. The personality of the adolescent, already partially developed during the formative years (from approximately two to six years old) is now being discovered and experimented with. Many adolescents are very dissatisfied with how they look (an estimated eighty per cent are unhappy with their appearance) and with what kind of a person they are. This dissatisfaction automatically impinges itself upon their emotional reactions and development. Inconsistency emerges as some aspects of adolescence are enjoyed to the full (with new experiences and new emotions being indulged for their own sake), whilst other aspects of adolescence are clearly disliked.

A survey done across 150 Christian youth groups, embracing eight denominations and covering 1,729 young people, indicates something of the extent of this negative emotional reaction directed by adolescents towards themselves. Asked to score themselves out of a possible top mark of three in each of the following categories, the scores proved remarkably low: the average score for adolescents assessing themselves to be kind was 1.2; to be intelligent was 0.7; and to be popular was 0.6. This does indicate the insecurity and inferiority prevalent in the emotional development of many adolescents, and is a further reason why their emotions are so inconsistent – all too often the adolescents' likes and dislikes are at war, not only externally, but within themselves. Their personalities are in a state of flux, and often in an attempt to discover their identity adolescents will embark upon a series of 'role plays'. These take the form of assumed characters (perhaps observed from TV/sports/music idols), and the roles being played are often very different. They might be heavily macho and aggressive, and at the next moment very caring and sensitive. The roles or masks hide the identity of the true adolescent; they are often not a deliberate attempt to do so, but rather an attempt on the part of the adolescent to experiment with the feelings associated with that role model. Role models are therefore more an attempt to stretch emotional experience rather than hide emotional identity. They may also be an attempt to adopt attitudes which will gain them perceived access to a much coveted peer group or gang. Whichever way, discovery of identity provides another basis for emotional inconsistencies in the life of the adolescent.

Despite the complexities involved thus far in understanding the world of the adolescent, I have consistently found it encouraging in my work amongst young people as a schools worker, youth worker, trainer and developer (and latterly as a father!) to realise that particularly in the realm of emotional development the adolescent is not *always* looking for people who can explain everything, or even understand everything. The heartfelt cry of many an adolescent may well be: 'You just don't understand!' — but when in the midst of emotional change and crisis, the adolescent is both looking for and can recognise people who will themselves provide positive, warm, supportive and encouraging emotional support. The dictum holds true: 'They don't care how much you know until they know how much you care.'

CHAPTER EIGHT

'I THINK, THEREFORE . . .'

– THE MENTAL DEVELOPMENT OF THE ADOLESCENT

Up until the age of approximately seventeen or eighteen the number of brain cells in an individual's head is still increasing. After the age of seventeen or eighteen, several thousand brain cells die each day. Before you try (as I have in the past) to make excuses for your strange behaviour because of this fact, it is worth remembering that no human being uses more than a small percentage of their brain's potential anyway. However, it does mean that for the first half of adolescence the brain is still increasing in its potential capacity, and it is certainly true that areas of perception within the thinking and intellect of the average adolescent are being constantly expanded by both experience and education.

Questions, questions!

It is perhaps unfortunate, though it seems unavoidable, that into the midst of this intellectual and mental experimentation and stimulation come some of life's greatest decisions and challenges. Adolescents will be called upon to make quite critical decisions concerning what they want out of both their present and future lifestyles. Thus decisions will face them concerning family life: to follow the educational patterns set by previous generations, or perhaps become the 'first to go to university', to accept or reject the thought-through processes and world beliefs of the family, to stay at home or to leave, and so on. They also face decisions concerning morality, choices based on mental processes, not merely on emotional ones: should the adolescent lie, steal, cheat, indulge in homosexual experimentation, indulge in heterosexual experimentation, and so on. And adolescents may face a degree of mental turmoil in: seeking the approval of their peers, whether or not they should continue to attend church if they have been brought up to do so, whether or not they even believe in God, whether they wish to get married sooner, later or if at all, what road they wish to pursue concerning a career or further training, and of course the challenge of a success/failure-orientated education system. All of these life decisions demand mental processes and come at a time when advice from adults is not often easily sought or accepted.

The education system seems intent on bringing in the further pressures of examinations throughout the course of the adolescent's school life, often at critical stages of adolescent development. And so at thirteen adolescents are having to decide what courses to take which could map out their eventual destiny in terms of further education and a career. At fifteen they are taking GCSEs. At seventeen or eighteen they may be taking A-levels. At the same time they will need to be making decisions concerning further education: college, university, teacher training. It is unfortunately true that for many adolescents the challenge of the education system and the mental processes required to come to solutions and decisions actually breeds a terrible fear of failure. If this is combined with projected expectations and standards set by aspiring parents, the results can be quite traumatic. Written assessment and curriculum development in our schools (as with GCSEs) may well remove some of the pressure of final examinations through a process of continual assessment, but they have certainly increased the workload expected of adolescents at the age of about fourteen and fifteen. Because the mental development of adolescents incorporates a search for self-identity and worth, with the attendant feelings of insecurity and the need for constant affirmation, it will readily be understood that for some the pressures and workload of critical examinations at such a time of flux is counter-productive. Examination results can be affected severely by the onslaught of kakihaphiophobia, a chronic fear of failure.

A mental breather?

A number of child psychologists, perhaps best represented by Erik Erikson, have posited the observation that adolescence is a kind of stop-over place between childhood and adulthood, a kind of interruption of the normal flow of development, where individuals pause to gather mental, intellectual, emotional, physical and social reserves (almost to catch his or her breath as it were) before continuing on to maturing adulthood. The theory is that in this waiting room of adolescence the individual ego secures a synthesis by observation and experience of those around him or her, and then determines a direction, through a series of conscious and subconscious choices, which will ultimately determine firstly their identity, and secondly their destiny.

Even if this is a true reflection of adolescence, it is worth noting that development does not occur in a vacuum. The 'waiting room' of adolescence has a well stocked table of media influence, with certain adolescent themes running throughout, catering very expertly to the average teenager's mental development. The various forms of media (TV, video, music, etc) target adolescents, have a vast following, and often have a dominant theme of escape and unreality. This theme has been noted by Christian youth writer and evangelist John Allan and certainly seems to be backed up by the predominance of adolescents involved in various role play games which proliferate on the market (perhaps the most famous in the late-seventies and throughout the eighties being Dungeons and Dragons).

The appeal of such TV, radio, magazine, and game board content is two-fold. Firstly, because of the mental processes that adolescents are going through, they are seeking to determine a variety of roles before distinguishing their own identities. Secondly, the mental development of adolescents is marked by the beginning of philosophical arguments. These lead adolescents away from perceiving people and situations merely in concrete terms and develop an ability in them to think in terms that are more abstract and theoretical. Imagination, fantasy and word play are all involved in this mental development. The child's world of the immediate becomes the adolescent's world of the possible. The purely subjective actions and reactions of the child begin to take on something of the objectivity of adulthood through the process of adolescence. The preoccupation with the possible and the external leads adolescents into experimentation, both in their thought processes and in their actions. This can, of course, lead to the adolescent tension between a thought process and a conclusion, an ideal firmly held and yet not experientially tested.

Attempts to regulate the learning process of adolescents have been made throughout history. The philosopher Aristotle's observations indicate that in his time consideration *was* given to the development of adolescents, but Aristotle suggests that little space should be given to developing an educational programme where lifestyle is best suited to their psychological needs. Rather, Aristotle's priority in education was to give attention to the study of mathematics, astronomy and the theory of music, as these subjects enhanced development in abstract thought processes, but did not require the life experiences and wisdom necessary for adolescents to enter Aristotle's 'adult' world, epitomised for him by the role of either philosopher or physicist. This artificially divorces thought life from lifestyle, a typically Greek phenomenon. The problem with this, of course, is that adolescents are not in essence searching for a theoretical (or even theological) outlook, but are rather searching for an experientially based philosophy which fulfils their needs and gives answers to various key questions, which the mental development of adolescents starts to throw up at this time. Mental development and lifestyle, conclusions and consequences all need to be interrelated for the healthy mental development of adolescents. Indeed, this is the Jewish Rabbinic model of development and is akin to Jesus' New Testament means of discipleship.

It is important to recognise that whilst this process is *beginning* in adolescence, their mental development is not the same as that of adults in terms of their understanding, their expression (ability to communicate) and their experience. In early adolescence physical development makes it easy to realise that these people are not yet adults. In late adolescence growth spurts and physical development may fool us into thinking that they *are* adults.

More subtly (because it isn't physically observable) exactly the same trap awaits the adults watching the mental development of adolescents. Let the reader beware! The mental processes of adolescents are in flux and development just as much as the physical, social, emotional and social aspects investigated in other chapters of this book. None of us would now hold to the mediaeval view of a child's development, which stated that the essential difference between a child and an adult was a quantitative and not a qualitative one. Then, children were viewed as mini-adults, to be dressed in the same clothes, with the same interests, and therefore meriting the same treatment whereby adult rquirements will be placed upon the children and enforced by strong discipline. Under this theory of pre-formationism a child does not develop, but is rather pre-formed. This theory even surfaced in contemporary mediaeval embryology under the title of homunculism.

> It was seriously believed that the diminutive, but fully formed little man (ie, a homunculus) was embodied in the sperm and when implanted in the uterus, simply grew in bulk without any differentiation of tissue or organs, until full term foetal size was obtained at the end of nine months.
>
> (W. Hasley, *Changes in British Society*.)

Although we would not now go to such lengths, our regard for the mental processes of adolescence can fall into the same trap, whereby we expect a mature and adult response from people whose mental processes are still in a state of flux and development.

Concrete to abstract

This development of the beginning of abstract or philosophical thoughts and arguments has been observed by a number of important educational psychologists. Piaget estimated that the transition of concrete thought to abstract processes takes place around the age of eleven to twelve years, which is to say, just into the beginning of adolescence.

Ronald Goldman, with specific reference to the teaching of religious education in schools, put it a little later at about thirteen years, and typified it by examining the descriptions of God given by such young adolescents. Around this age God seems to become a figure described more by values than by appearance. He becomes a more indeterminate and abstract spirit force, rather than the picture portrayed by biblical literalism and popular mythology which could lend him the figure of a kind of benevolent Father Christmas on a cloud!

Goldman also points out that as adolescents begin to grapple with these concepts, the less able (with slower or lower mental development) will tend to move to a position of indifference or even hostility towards the concept of God, as they lose the belief in the literal interpretation of an old man in the sky, yet fail to grasp the implications of abstract theoretical and theological thought processes. A similar mental reaction against the concept of God might also result not from an inability to grasp the possibility of a God who cannot be seen and does not live in the clouds, but rather can be a reaction caused by the adolescents' inability to assemble and communicate language of sufficient complexity to communicate their thoughts on this matter. This is a scenario which I have encountered many times in the past, where adolescents have a keener and instinctive grasp of the concept of a God who carries personality and yet is Spirit, but find themselves unable to express these thoughts without the risk of severe ridicule from other adolescents (who are often equally insecure in their thought processes).

About turn

Loukes, a child education development psychologist, also makes a telling observation concerning an abrupt 'about turn' in the mental processes of many adolescents during the course of their education. Loukes suggests that a part of the process of leaving childhood behind is a deliberate rejection of previous education now felt by the adolescent to have been childish. Education of children which exposes them to ideas rather than imposes them might go some way towards diffusing this adolescent rejection of previous education, but it is certainly true that much education of children still takes place along the lines of authoritarian literalism, not least because the young mind thinks in concrete rather than abstract terms. Father Christmas and the tooth fairy, once unquestionably accepted by the child, become objects of scorn in the mental processes of adolescents. Similarly, Bible stories of Adam and Eve and Noah's ark, once unquestioned in the formative years, are frequently rejected in the adolescent years.

Adolescents will have a tendency to turn previous literal authoritarianism into contemporary liberal relativism. Awash in a sea of often conflicting emotions adolescents will frequently become by default existentialists (as noted by psychologist Kitwood) because they are looking for a philosophy of life which can be validated by their own personal experience. Thus, what is felt precedes what is; experience precedes essence, then relativism creeps in, whereby, 'If it works for you that's okay, but it may not work for me.' And so my truth cannot automatically become true for the adolescent who is searching for his or her own truths and set of experiences. If I seek to impose my truth upon the adolescent then I am representative once again of the adult authoritarian literalism which the adolescent will tend consciously or subconsciously to associate with the childhood from which he or she is seeking to escape.

This may all seem rather negative for the claims of Christianity in the mental processes of the average adolescent! This, however, is not the whole picture concerning their mental development, and it is certainly not the whole picture concerning their spiritual development, which we will investigate in Chapters 11 to 13. This is because key questions are being thrown up by the mental development of adolescents. Anyone who is living with, bringing up, teaching, or working with young people, needs to do so with the assurance that such questions *are* being asked at whatever level of mental or academic ability exists in the life of the adolescent. Moreover, we need to find out what those existentially important questions are which are alive in the heart and mind of that adolescent. Tillich (to quote another educational psychologist) points out the need not only to identify such important questions, but also to encourage radical questioning, since a mental decision with moral implications upon the adolescent's lifestyle is only of real value when the alternatives to those decisions have been thoroughly looked at and the cost counted. In fact, biblically this is one of the prerequisites of discipleship (Lk 14:28), and Scripture consistently places a high value upon our need for a renewed mind (Rom 12:1–2), upon the battle which goes on for our minds (Eph 6:17), and upon the importance of our thinking shaping our behaviour (2 Cor 10:5, Prov 23:7, Phil 4:8).

Erik Erikson puts forward seven characteristics of the mental development of adolescents through puberty, as follows:

1. Inner disorganisation.
2. Preparation for adulthood through attempts at integration.
3. A religious feeling for life which is bound up with reflection about such things as: loneliness, love, death and God.
4. Forming a new plan for life.
5. Growing into the world of older people.
6. Finding oneself and one's place in the world.
7. Search for identification and ideology.

Note that point three of Erikson's outline goes some way towards identifying what these existentially important questions are, which are vibrant in the hearts and minds of adolescents. It would be by identifying with such adolescent themes, by asking questions about them as well as posing answers, by using concrete illustrations on these themes and yet being prepared to move to the more abstract in terms of how such themes impinge themselves upon our own experiences (which is why shared testimony works well with adolescents), that we can begin to make helpful inroads into the mental development of young people.

Much of what we have outlined in this chapter takes place on a subliminal level, and it is often only the surface waves that indicate the extent of mental turmoil going on deep below the surface. Much of this development is *not* negative, but it is involved. Helping adolescents understand and come to terms with what is going on in their thought processes is itself very valid, but we will need to find ways in through the surface waves before we can deal with what is going on in the depths! That will require us always to remember that adolescents will be prone to mood swings, which in turn will affect and be affected by their thought processes. We will need to remember that the average concentration span of an adolescent is somewhere between ten to fifteen minutes. We must at all costs avoid patronising young people, either by our approach (authoritarian literalism) or by our content (too concrete and not sufficiently abstract and philosophical).

We will also need to remember that whatever we say may well be subject to word play. Philologists do not yet understand whether in the development of very young children speech patterns and rhythms precede cognition or whether the reverse is true. Despite the work of linguists and philologists such as Noam Chomsky, we still cannot comprehend how the human mind can form and interpret spoken and written communication at the rate of which it is capable. But we certainly do understand that in adolescence experimentation begins to take place with the means and processes of communication, and consequently whatever you say to an adolescent may well be subject to word plays, double entendre, the most awful word puns and a prevalence towards anarchistic humour (easy to assess by examining the nature of an adolescent's favourite TV comedies and comedians, often anti-authoritarian). During adolescence the beginning of play with ideas will in itself be enough to excite the mind and actions of the adolescent, and all too often the attraction is to the excitement rather than to the idea! All of these are factors which need to be taken into consideration concerning the mental development of adolescents, particularly when we come to look at subjects such as youth evangelism in Chapter 13.

In the next chapter we will begin to examine the social interaction of adolescents.

CHAPTER NINE

GET IT TOGETHER

– THE SOCIAL DEVELOPMENT
OF THE ADOLESCENT

Previous chapters have sought to determine the development of adolescents through interrelated areas of change. None of these areas can be viewed in isolation, hence the processes of mental and emotional development can have a profound effect on the social life of adolescents. So too, though perhaps to a lesser extent, may physical development. The girl who at fourteen looks her age when in school uniform, may very well look eighteen or more when dressed up for an evening's dancing at the local discothèque, or an evening's under-age drinking at the local pub. The sporting prowess of a healthy sixteen-year-old boy may mean that much of his social development is done in the context of the local football team or mountain bike club. The emergence of a young man's baritone from a small boy's treble (combined with the attraction of a pretty blonde in the chorus line, as was the case for the author!) may mean that social life revolves around the local amateur operatic society!

Recognising the overlap in these areas of change, it will be helpful to look at some of the social trends prevalent amongst such adolescents. Such trends have the added benefit of indicating to the reader what some of the key influences are upon the overall development of adolescents; how, where and why some adolescents find (and identify with) their peer groups, and how media and advertising conspire, along with many forms of recreation, to part adolescents from their money. I will for the sake of inclusion cover such topics as drug abuse (including cigarette and alcohol consumption) in the course of this chapter, under the general (if unfortunate) heading of 'recreation'. In order to better understand what motivates and drives adolescents we will look primarily in this chapter at those aspects of socialising which emerge from, and to a degree shape, the individual's character and attitudes. We will therefore, of necessity, be looking at social development outside the context of work and education. This chapter aims to investigate what adolescents *prefer* to do, rather than that which an employment or education system enforces upon them.

Of course, a primary factor in such social development is time available. At present our society is still suffering from the effects of the worst economic recession for fifty or more years. The latest government statistics indicate a very high level of unemployment, even allowing for seasonal (valid or otherwise, depending upon your viewpoint) adjustment, and at the time of writing stands at 2.75 million people. The effects of long-term unemployment can be devastating in the inherent statement that it makes, in our success orientated society, on the value and worth of an individual and his or her right to work. It also has a very practical effect, in terms of the amount of time available to that individual, on socialising (which will be at a maximum), whilst having a very negative effect upon the amount of finance that individual has available to him or her for such socialising (which will be at a minimum).

In 1975 sixty per cent of all sixteen-year-olds were in full-time employment. By 1988, at the time of the last published census results, only twenty-two per cent of all sixteen-year-olds who had left school were involved in full-time employment. This despite the fact that there were one per cent fewer teenagers in 1988 than in 1975. It is quite clear that large scale unemployment has affected teenagers disproportionately to any other group. In spite of the fact that in 1988 more teenagers stayed on at school, thirty per cent of all those who didn't went on government sponsored youth training schemes and subsequently into unemployment. Figures comparing the situation for teenagers two years after leaving school hold little hope of consolation. Although by the age of eighteen seventy per cent of teenagers were involved in full-time employment, there was nevertheless a four hundred per cent increase of unemployed eighteen-year-olds between 1975 and 1988. The fifty per cent increase in those staying on for further education at eighteen is perhaps indicative of a lack of viable alternatives in terms of employment. These figures have their source in the Department of Education and Science, December 1988.

Our understanding of the social development of adolescents will be helped if we next investigate their values, both those stated and those inherent in the way adolescents spend their money and their time, whether employed or not. Much valuable survey work was done in a book entitled *Young Britain 1990*, and a survey amongst fifteen- to twenty-four-year-olds indicated that eighty-one per cent of them felt that the family unit was the single most important thing in their lives. Those in favour of hard work comprised ninety-four per cent, and sixty-seven per cent of them felt green issues were enormously important and were prepared to give time, money and commitment to them. A survey of the spending power of the same group indicated that most of their money was spent on visits to the pub, clothes, eating out, sexual activity, music tapes and cigarettes. A

Mintel poll in October 1991, amongst eleven- to sixteen-year-olds, gives an indication of material values and money spent when it highlights the fact that more than fifty per cent of those surveyed were in personal possession of a TV, a camera and a hi-fi system.

As one would expect, these indications of the social values of adolescents in the UK have a direct bearing on the way that such adolescents spend their social time. A Gallup poll in February 1989, taken of a large number of fifteen- to twenty-five-year-olds, indicated that ninety per cent of them listened to records at least once a week (a statistic increasingly equatable with tapes and CDs), with twenty-six per cent of them visiting a disco at least once a week, and fifty-two per cent of them watching a video or paying a visit to a cinema at least on a once-weekly basis. A Mintel poll in 1990 attempted to ascertain the frequency and type of recreation that teenagers were involved in, and discovered that thirteen- to twenty-four-year-olds would expect to socialise with friends at least twice a week, whilst fifty per cent of thirteen- to twenty-four-year-olds would expect to visit a pub with friends on at least a weekly basis. Socialising, and therefore social development, is clearly of great importance to young adults in the UK. A National Opinion Poll in September 1989 amongst sixteen- to twenty-five-year-olds further indicated how that group would best choose to enjoy their free time: fifty-five per cent of them would prefer either visiting friends or receiving visits from friends in their homes; fifty per cent would prefer to go out with their friends; and thirty-seven per cent of them would most naturally gravitate to the pub, with twenty-five per cent of them preferring shopping sprees, and fourteen per cent preferring sports activities. A mere four per cent of them preferred to spend their time socially at church.

In an age where much communication is at the audio-visual level it is unsurprising that the primary inheritors of this new age of communications should be spending considerable amounts of time watching TV and videos. Eighty-five per cent of seven- to seventeen-year-olds watch television on a daily basis, with twenty-six per cent of them watching it for four hours or more. The average teenager watches some twenty-four hours of television per week. Since teenagers form a large part of the uncommitted spending power of this country (spending some £18 million per week) it is not insignificant how TV advertisements are slanted, with eighty per cent of their content concentrating on the body (a source of great insecurity to the average adolescent), only eighteen per cent on the mind (obviously developing areas of the philosophical and abstract during adolescence, but as yet unable to attain a concentration span of much more than fifteen minutes), and only two per cent on the spirit (despite the fact that up to eighty per cent of young people in this country believe in God).

More than fifty per cent of all UK homes now own two or more television sets, with only two per cent having none at all. The UK leads the field in the percentage of video owning homes across Europe; by the end of 1988 sixty-three per cent of all UK homes had a video, and the estimate was that by 1998 that figure will have gone up to seventy-three per cent. An average of 7.5 hours of video viewing per week is in addition to the number of hours of TV watching. During a poll taken throughout the month of February 1988, it was discovered that thirty-three per cent of all sixteen- to twenty-four-year-olds had seen a minimum of one religious TV programme, which has to be an encouraging statistic for Christians working in the media and on the provisions of the Broadcasting Bill. In contrast, it is estimated that only seventeen per cent of teenagers read books or magazines on a 'prefer to' rather than a 'need to' basis (ie, books which are a mandatory part of a school or employment curriculum).

Social addicts?

Statistics indicate that the use and abuse of alcohol, tobacco and drugs is also a significant factor in the socialising of adolescents in the UK in recent years. The book *Youth in the 1990s* (UNESCO/HMSO) discovered that twenty-five per cent of teenagers under the age of eighteen were drinking alcohol regularly, with sixty per cent of them buying alcohol on a regular basis, thirty per cent of thirteen- to sixteen-year-olds drinking alcohol at least once a week. This despite the fact that a survey done in 1990 indicated that sixty per cent of fifteen- to twenty-four-year-olds considered alcohol to be a dangerous drug, and eighty-eight per cent maintaining that they would never drink and drive. None the less, the same survey revealed that thirty-three per cent spent a considerable amount of time in the pub, with twenty per cent of the males surveyed indicating that by the end of the evening they wanted to be drunk. On average, those surveyed spent £14 per week on alcohol.

Two years later a MORI poll taken among 7,000 sixteen- to nineteen-year-olds discovered that half of those polled (the older teenagers) had had a hangover, and half of those had been physically sick as a result of over-drinking. One in six of them had indulged in sexual activity on a one-night stand as a result of intoxication, and fifty-three per cent of them admitted to having at least one drink of alcohol a week. In the UK the heavier regular drinker is likely to be male, with the heaviest drinking being done by males from the age of eighteen to twenty-four. Males drink more than twice as much as females in the same category.

Although these figures do correlate, there seems to have been a decline between a survey done by the *Daily Express* in February 1989, the MORI Poll of 1992 and the *Daily Express* survey discovered that fifty per cent or more of fifteen- to twenty-five-year-olds surveyed drank neither beer nor lager, and seventy-five per cent of them drank neither wine nor spirits. A book which surveyed the social activities of young churched people in the 1980s produced rather more encouraging results: in the free churches sixty-six per cent of those interviewed felt that it was wrong to get drunk, although approximately the same numbers in the Roman Catholic and Anglican Church felt that there was nothing wrong with drinking alcohol.

It is important to remember that whilst statistical analysis of the recreational activities and social life of adolescents will vary (hopefully towards the positive!) when comparisons are made between the churched and the unchurched, none the less our church adolescents have to grow up within the same framework and society, and the peer group pressure upon them to experiment is just as great as upon their peers who are unchurched. It would be unrealistic of us to expect (and indeed surveys indicate otherwise) that there will be an *automatic* difference in the use of time, experimentation with drugs, alcohol and spending of finances between the young people in our churches as opposed to the majority of young people who are not in our churches. It is unfortunately still true that part of the reason for this is that many churches are not tackling the root issues that underline experimentation and which we have sought to understand in the various chapters of this book, and are consequently not teaching practical, relevant, lifestyle related material which gives God's and the church's reasonable, explained parameters when it comes to these issues. Thus there remains a direct correlation between what happens with unchurched young and what happens amongst churched youth; the same survey just mentioned amongst Christianised youth in the eighties indicated that thirty-seven per cent of Roman Catholics never read their Bibles, and neither did nineteen per cent of Anglican and free church young people. In the light of what we have just said this should not be surprising in a non-book youth culture (remember, only seventeen per cent read by preference). Such correlations do exist between churched and unchurched youth.

It remains something of a legal anomaly which has implications on the social recreation of young people that it is not illegal to smoke cigarettes at any age. It is, however, illegal to purchase cigarettes under the age of sixteen. None-the-less, twenty-five per cent of fourteen- to fifteen-year-olds smoke a minimum of one cigarette a week, and when the age range goes up so does the percentage, with thirty per cent of older teenagers smoking eleven or twelve cigarettes a day. The *Daily Express'* February 1989 survey of fifteen- to twenty-five-year-olds indicated that seventy-five per cent of them were non-smoking. General trends amongst youth smokers do still seem to indicate that whilst the overall number of smokers has significantly reduced, the amount of teenage female smoking is still increasing, perhaps as a backlash to society's previous perception that it was somehow unfeminine for women to smoke cigarettes. Whatever your view on cigarette smoking, it is quite clear from Scripture that addiction to anything is unacceptable, and perhaps all the more so when such addiction can be demonstrably proven to have a detrimental effect upon health. By the end of the 1980s tobacco was contributing to at least 100,000 premature deaths in the UK each year, with each cigarette on average being said to shorten the life of a habitual smoker by 5.5 minutes. And this before we even consider the environmental issues of tobacco production.

Unfortunately it is not only the manufacturers of clothes, records, bikes, cosmetics, and so on, who target the free floating cash of the average adolescent; it is also the soft and hard drug pushers, whose wares are far less socially acceptable than are the wares of brewery and tobacco barons. In comparison with the mid-seventies, by the middle of the eighties teenagers stood a 186 per cent greater chance of getting involved in persistent drug abuse.

Consequently, by the mid-1980s there were four times the number of under twenty-one-year-old registered drug addicts than there had been by the end of the 1970s. Compared over the same timescale, by the mid-eighties there were 12,500 narcotics drug addicts known to the Home Office in the UK, whilst in the mid-seventies there were only 3,500. There are now in excess of an estimated 50,000 heroin addicts in the UK.

In surveys on drug abuse which I have taken in schools ranging between East London and the south coast, approximately fifty per cent of any class will claim to know drug takers. Reasons given for the use of drugs include: boredom, the physical and mental pleasure and stimulation which they give, peer group pressure, rebellion against authority figures (school, church, parents), and curiosity is a big factor also. The survey mentioned earlier conducted amongst church youth in the 1980s, indicated that eighty per cent of those from a free church background thought that the use and abuse of cannabis was wrong. This again is an encouragingly higher proportion than that to be expected from the national average.

I have tried through the use of these statistics to indicate the social trends emerging across adolescents in the UK. On a general level, depending upon the age band into which they fall, social development amongst adolescents depends largely upon a gregarious peer group instinct and relationship experimentation, and is often centred around music, fashion and sporting activities, with hobbies also as a significant factor. Not all of the factors which I have listed here are necessarily bad ones; we will need to identify the pressures, positive and negative, upon the lives of adolescents if we are to better understand them, be enabled to reach out to them with clearly explained parameters and provide socially relevant alternatives both in the life of the family and in the extended church family.

In perhaps no other sphere is the interrelationship of

other areas of development of greater importance. Thus, social expression is both a reflection and a product of the physical, mental, emotional, and spiritual development of the adolescent.

There remain to us three specific spheres where we need to earth our understanding of adolescents at all of these levels, including the social aspect. These are, in the order we will deal with them: the family, the church and the unchurched.

CHAPTER TEN

LET GO AND LET GROW

– YOUNG PEOPLE AND YOUR FAMILY

There can be no area where the reality of your walk with God and the motivations of your heart in terms of bringing up adolescents will be more severely tested than in the family home. It is here that you will see your son or daughter, or your extended family member, at his or her best and worst. It is here that they will see you at yours! This is the realm (I hesitate to say arena!) in which theories fly out of the window and reality, sometimes harsh, makes itself felt on a day-to-day basis in the life of the family unit. The home and home life carries so much potential for the positive development of adolescents that it becomes all the more crucial that we have understood what is going on internally and externally in the development of adolescents thus far. By the time we get into the joys and frustrations of family life it will be too late then to attempt further theorising. By that stage, whatever we do not understand we will tend to fear or react against, and as the family life comes closest to us and has the potential of catching us unawares and at our most vulnerable, it is all the more vital that we have done our homework in applying all that we have learned thus far into the family scene.

Being a relatively new parent, I will content myself in this chapter with outlining, under a series of practical headings, a number of areas of potential growth and/or conflict. These I have gained from my own experience of being brought up in a family home which consistently demonstrated love and care, without a lack of structure and discipline, but not without its own problems. My grateful thanks for this obviously go to my parents. My observations also come from the occasions when I have been an external arbiter (with the permission of parents and adolescents) in a number of cases evolving from my working with teenagers over the course of the last fourteen years. In very few of the following scenarios are there definitive answers or a 'right way' of doing things, but I can at least hope that the suggestions which I make are practical and workable, and may be used as some kind of guideline or framework for you to depart from, if adjustments are needed. I have jotted these thoughts down in note form under a series of obvious headings so that you can refer to any section you need to, as occasion demands!

Housework

There is a fine balance to be drawn between serving and loving the individual adolescent in his or her home environment, and encouraging him or her to grow in maturity and responsibility, so that that environment is not taken for granted as a kind of perpetual home room service provided by parents for their offspring. Tip the balance and you find parents who treat their children as sources of income and of cheap labour, which is extremely exploitative and far from caring and loving. The practical outworking of this parental attitude ranges from the expectation of the adolescent to act as a kind of inbuilt gardener/decorator/dishwasher/babysitter. Tip the balance the other way and the contribution of the adolescent to home life is totally minimised, with the young person perpetually taking from the family unit, rather than giving to it. This is disastrous when it comes to teaching the adolescent responsibility, thoughtfulness, sacrifice, and value of time, energy and money. It is also a disastrous model which will reproduce itself into the next generation, ie, any future children of your own son or daughter. It is not a model that should be perpetuated. Biblical love wants the best for the other person, and it is not best to allow that person to be indolent, lazy, self-centred or irresponsible.

Of course individuals – which includes mothers and fathers – work in different ways, and not every household is organised into time structures and cleaning rotas. But I do have to say that those in the best organised households that I have come across do have some rudimentary ideas of job descriptions and timespans within which jobs need to be done. I think of the busy lives of a family in our church with three adolescent daughters, where the father is a solicitor and housegroup leader; the mother is a local councillor, a teacher and one of our congregation's leaders. Yet the family life is well run, delegated and very loving. It seems to me that within this there is the opportunity to teach adolescents about time and diary management and about self-discipline. Certainly I would favour a distribution of jobs among adolescent teenagers (I think that five is about the minimum and thirteen is an objective maximum age at which to start distributing jobs and responsibility in the household), with the jobs worked out, wherever possible, on the basis of (a) preference, ie what does the adolescent actually want to do, and (b) time taken for each job, since time is one of the adolescent's most valuable commodities. It may be necessary for other factors to be taken into consideration, such as responsibility levels – it is clearly a more responsible job to be in charge of your five-year-old sister than it is to mow the lawn. Jobs which would lend themselves well to a rota system obviously include setting and clearing tables, cooking, washing up, changing beds, doing the washing, hanging out and bringing in the laundry, ironing, shopping and errands, car cleaning, lawn and garden maintenance, dusting and hoovering, and baby-sitting.

I would include as a job the adolescent keeping his or her bedroom reasonably tidy, though I feel it is important that choice of decor (wallpaper, curtains, colours, carpet, posters, room layout, etc) are important decisions to leave in the hands of the adolescent. However, I would not be in favour of the adolescent alone being responsible for cleaning his or her room on a regular basis, unless he or she so desires out of a sense of maintaining territory and privacy. The reason for this is that I would prefer to see all bedrooms in general cleaned as part of the household duties, thus extending a sense of sharing beyond that of mere territory. 'I'll clean my bedroom and no one else's,' is not a helpful attitude! It is difficult to maintain a fair and reasonable explanation as to why the adolescent must dust and hoover his or her own bedroom, whilst the other bedrooms are done as part of the normal household chores. It ought of course to be noted that as with all forms of development, leadership must be by example, and therefore the housework and household chores need to be divided across the whole family, with allowances being made for hours worked by mother or father as necessary.

Multimedia

Both television and videos come with their internalised censorship rating. Videos carry clear markings and usually an explanation of those markings on the tape itself (U, PG, 15, 18), and the general rule of thumb for television producers is that material of the 18 rating will not be shown on television until after 9.00 pm. In younger life these guidelines are helpful and can be imposed externally by parents, but the goal to aim at for adolescent life is that an internal switch is built into the conscience and willpower of the adolescent to help him or her self-determine the levels of censorship needed, for purposes of wisdom, morality and appropriateness. No such censorship is inherent within the music industry, other than when records are banned by the BBC. With many adolescents now owning their own TV and stereo systems, and most with access at least to their parents' video cassette recorders, the possibilities for abuse and harmful exposure to audio or audio-visual material is very high. The bottom line must remain – that for as long as the adolescent lives in the household of his or her mother and father, it is the parents' wishes and taste that must prevail.

Reasons for the exercise of censorship should always be explained if necessary in conjunction with viewing such material to be censored, rather than acrimonious shouting matches over whose house it is and who pays the TV licence! Placing yourself under obligation to the adolescents by asking them to explain to you what they would like to see, with sample copies, will be a helpful way of establishing this kind of internal censorship switch within them, as will affirmation of their right to say no, and the exercise of their willpower over and above peer group pressure. This is important since many of the problems arise not only in your own household, but when your adolescent progeny are in the homes of their friends or the parents of their friends, where standards may very well be different.

Issues like the volume of music played in bedrooms can be a constant source of confrontation, since most stereos (like the potential speed of many cars) are designed to cater for volume levels well above the comfortable! Emulating live concert sound in the confines of a small bedroom can potentially produce friction (and earache!). An appeal to thoughtful consideration for others (or surrounding houses!) is a starting point, though pragmatically it might also be helpful to look at ways forward with the adolescent to better soundproof his or her room. I remember embarking on a project with my father, where together we provided fairly effective soundproofing insulation around my room in order to help reduce such causes of friction. Encouraging the adolescent, perhaps on a fifty-fifty basis, to save up towards the cost of a decent pair of stereo headphones might be another way forward, particularly where gimmicks are involved such as infra-red remote headphones which do not require a lead.

A number of parents express concern at the amount of finance being spent on music equipment, records, tapes and CDs. Most of us are fortunate enough to have a degree of money to spend on our own hobbies or pastimes, and it is relatively easy for any of us to denigrate those of others whilst turning a blind eye to our own. My wife and I enjoy dining out occasionally in good restaurants, which necessitates us spending money that others would be horrified to spend on a meal. However, some of our friends might invest their spare cash into disco or fishing equipment, CD or video collections, or TV satellite dishes. It really comes down to a matter of taste and conscience. The taste is down to the individual, and conscience needs to be educated and developed in the life of the adolescent.

Therefore, spending on CDs and tapes needs to be weighed in the context of the overall spending power of adolescents. Are they also giving a percentage of their money to a more selfless cause, such as a worth while charity which stimulates their altruistic nature? If the adolescents are Christians, are they as a minimum tithing their income? If the adolescents are actually earning money, as opposed to simply receiving pocket money, has it been considered that they may be able to make a small (but none-the-less proportionally representative) contribution towards the cost of their upkeep? Such financial matters will help the teenager understand the value of money, of self-discipline, the pitfalls of credit and the virtues of patience.

Money

I have in the last section touched on some issues concerning finance. I would encourage the provision of pocket money from a relatively early age, in order that the adolescent can soon learn the value of money, the cause and effect of desire and gratification of desire, the self-discipline of saving and the sacrifice of giving. I am not in favour of financial rewards for jobs done around the house. This seems to me to foster a performance based approach to supply and demand, and to promote a concept of automatic reward, which is not verified by the adolescent's other experiences of life, and nor does it foster a generous spirit. The rate at which pocket money is given must of course depend upon the available finances of the family unit, including monies needing to be given to other children. Overall family budgeting and sharing should *not* be kept a secret.

I do feel that adolescence, or perhaps the turning of teens, needs to mark a more significant increase in spending money which will now be going towards make-up, magazines, CDs and hobbies, where once it only went on sweets at the local shop. It is invidious to seek to put a figure on how much should be given, although I would be tempted to suggest the principle that if a thirteen-year-old wants to collect CDs – which cost £15 a time – he or she ought to learn the value of saving three to seven weeks' pocket money in order to be able to buy them. I stress the principle and not the figure.

The three areas where I would want to encourage financial responsibility in all adolescents, from pocket money or earnings accrued by their part-time/Saturday jobs, would be: (a) that adolescents learn the value of regular saving, and I would encourage the use of a building society or bank account; (b) that if the adolescents profess Christian faith, they learn the value of tithing a minimum ten per cent, and whether or not a Christian commitment is professed, they should learn the value of generous giving to worthy causes; and (c) that some proportional consideration is given towards housekeeping and upkeep costs.

Any friend of yours . . .

I can remember the sense of belonging to the family unit – the solid base for building friendships, and of pride in my parents, which my mother and father's clear acceptance of my own friends engendered within me. There was a vocalised and often affirmed understanding that any friends of mine, whether male or female, were welcome in the family home at any time. Obviously, convenience was a factor, but it usually *was* convenient. And so the home was available to me to bring people back for dinner, for overnight stays, for weekend visits, or to go on holiday with us, as the level of friendship dictated. This seems to me to be a healthy rule of thumb to be adopted by parents for their adolescent children. It will be the case, of course, that extending this level of welcome and freedom will mean that people visit your home whom you would not naturally choose to have associate with your offspring! Ultimately, of course, the choice is your offspring's and not yours. The ground rules here seem to be that friends are accepted and welcomed, but whilst they are in the confines of your own home you can reasonably expect them to abide by the rules which you ask of other members of the family, which of course includes the person who invited them in the first place!

This kind of open-handed, but gently firm acceptance, gives you the advantage of seeing the friends whom your adolescent son or daughter is making, and of exploring if necessary at a later date what it is that attracts him or her to them, and whether if there are any obvious shortcomings, these have been recognised rather than emulated. This also gives parents the added advantage of knowing where their offspring has gone when the time comes for the young person to visit the homes of his or her friends, to stay overnight or weekends, or to embark on holidays. In early adolescence, contact between you and the parents of your children's friends on a face-to-face basis is, I would suggest, vital in this day and age. Subsequently, at the least telephone calls or written communication would be of value. And certainly from my own experience strong friendships have built up between my parents and the parents of some of my friends, which have lasted through the years. When it comes to overnight stays it does, however, remain vital that we know whom our offspring are staying with, why they are staying overnight, where that is, with a contact number and address, and finally, that we exercise a measure of trust to our progeny!

Time, please!

Perhaps nothing causes such titanic clashes in family life than the subject of when the adolescent should be back home. It seems generally true to me that most adolescents feel they need more space than they actually do to grow into adulthood in the context of the family, while most parents think that they need less room than they actually do to make that transition. The general rule of thumb therefore is to give space, to let go and let grow. This is true of all of the subjects that we have covered thus far and that we will do in this chapter. And it is also true of the subject of time. However, the responsibility of the parent also necessitates taking into consideration the kind of age and society in which we live, and the dangers which are very real for any young person out late at night.

Neither children nor adolescents can be kept living in cotton-wool for fear of what might happen. On this basis they would never have been brought into the world at all. It is better to create a basis for wise and good decisions, than to seek constantly to impose external regulations. The biblical concept of the weaker brother in Romans 14, is that we do not continue perpetually to cater to his weakness, but rather that by doing so initially we earn enough room and right to lead them from weakness to strength. There is no virtue in perpetual weakness, immaturity or externally imposed regulations. The same applies in the growth and development of adolescents.

My own feeling is that the provision of a key at the age of about fifteen is a good sign of trust from parent to adolescent, and the key word for timings thereafter needs to be flexibility according to circumstance. It seems to me that a series of fail-safe devices, rather than one categorical time limit, is a more helpful way forward. Thus, at age sixteen years it might be felt that an 11 pm curfew would be normative, with a phone call or an explanation if that is going to stretch to 11.30 pm, and an absolute extension, which should have been arranged beforehand, of midnight for special situations like parties. A good rule of thumb is to work backwards from the morning hours. If the adolescent has to be out of bed at 7.30 am in order to wash, eat breakfast, and be out of the house for 8.00 am to catch a school bus, then eight hours of sleep or rest would necessitate a curfew of 11–11.30 pm. Explained parameters and encouragement of the adolescent to recognise his or her own tiredness factors will be a help in deciding all of these things, and time limits are best agreed upon rather than imposed.

Have wheels, will travel!

It is in my opinion a mistake to provide an adolescent with a car or motor-bike at too early a stage. In fact the provision of such a vehicle needs at the very least to be a joint endeavour between parents and adolescent (practically, for the adolescent this will often have to be the case because of the initial outlay), but this is an excellent opportunity for the adolescent to learn the value of patience and saving when it comes to driving lessons, vehicle tax, insurance and maintenance.

In the interim, before he or she acquires a vehicle (and I have to confess, I would always personally steer them towards a car and away from a motor-bike, which I consider to be dangerous to any user), lies the possibility of borrowing the family car. Again, here there is much room for negotiation and discussion between all parties involved concerning frequency, timings, petrol money, contribution to insurance and maintenance. In a household of mother, father and two adolescents, where all drive, flexibility needs to be the keynote. Real flexibility will, on occasion, inconvenience the adolescents, and on occasion the parents. Parental commitment to lending the car should be, whilst readily forthcoming, restricted to an 'ad hoc' basis of usually no more than one week in advance. The parents retain at all times control and arbitration between their children, and the sense of 'right to use' is thus helpfully avoided. In most cases it ought to be sufficient to impress upon the borrowing adolescent the need to refill the car with petrol to its original level, rather than simply hand over money which is its equivalent.

I would certainly be in favour of encouraging adolescents to learn to drive in a responsible manner by means of initial lessons taught within the family, but finishing lessons should be taught by a reputable driving instructor. Cost of the lessons and driving test can be subsidised fifty/fifty between parent and adolescent. I would recommend that such a course is embarked upon at the earliest opportunity (ie, at seventeen with the granting of a provisional licence).

Alcoholic bar?

It is of course illegal for young people to consume alcohol on licensed premises under the age of sixteen years, although they may enter pubs once they are fourteen, and at any age under that providing it is in the context of a family room and they're not drinking alcohol. At the age of sixteen non alcoholic drinks may be bought at a bar, and wine may be drunk on licensed premises with a meal, but not otherwise. At the age of eighteen the restrictions are rescinded and alcohol can be both bought and consumed. For as long as these are the laws of the land and there are no moral reasons why they should not be adhered to they must be adhered to (Rom 13). Explanations of law-keeping, and law-making, can be discussed with adolescents quite separately from the context of alcohol, but must be applied to that subject. Again, reasonable and explained parameters are clearly the way forward in the matter, as in many others, and biblical commands and wisdom can be appealed to if the adolescent professes Christian faith (ie, Eph 5:18, Gal 5:21). Demonstrated moderation from a parental position is also a key factor in alcohol consumption. And since personally I can find nothing biblically or experientially wrong with the moderate drinking of alcohol for social and pleasure purposes, I would not seek to impose abstinence upon my children. Legally they can drink alcohol in the home context over the age of five, under that for medicinal purposes only.

What I would want my children to understand are the dangers of excess (both socially, medically, and morally) and the horrendous cost to society that alcohol abuse produces (in terms of premature death, alcoholism, car crashes, immoral and often illegal liaisons and unwanted pregnancies). I would also want to teach them to appreciate the positive values of alcohol and to treat it with pleasure and respect. Certainly in earlier days a part of that respect would be the physical locking away of the household's wines and spirits, although with advanced adolescence I might want to negotiate that as a clearly demonstrated trust in the increasing responsibility and maturity of that adolescent.

The dating game

Dating, at least on a social basis, is likely to start taking place from around the age of twelve upwards, though it is not uncommon for people to have their first boy/girlfriend at the age of fourteen/fifteen. It would be my opinion that anything but the mildest of teasing from parents on this area is out of order, as this is a very sensitive area in the development of a young person, and the adolescent's respective boy/girlfriend should be invited home, not in any heavy way, but in order to meet him or her and encourage the friendship. I would also seek to encourage the friendship in the context of other people, so that protracted sessions alone, and particularly in rooms with beds in them (!), are avoided. Communication with the adolescent, and at a time which is slightly more remote from the subject in hand, is critical in this area as in many others, and the more open the channels of communication can be kept the better.

The average amount of time spent by boys talking to their fathers, and by girls talking to their mothers, and vice versa, over the course of a normal day is horrifying. In a survey conducted across more than 1,700 churched young people (representing 150 youth groups and eight denominations), sons spent an average of three minutes talking to their fathers and four minutes to their mothers, with daughters spending an average of 3.5 minutes talking to their fathers and 6.5 minutes to their mothers, per day! Obviously, this is less than healthy. This is not a total reflection of how much time is spent with the young person. The same survey indicated, on a score from nought (never) to three (frequently), that the average response to the question, 'Are your parents really interested in what you are doing?' was 2.4, and to parental time spent with the adolescent, 2.2.

Communication and important issues are what need to be worked upon, rather than simply time spent together.

The issue is clearly not merely one of quantity, but of quality.

Of the same group, thirty-five per cent obtained most of their sex education from friends, with thirty-one per cent deriving it from school, and twenty per cent of them obtaining most of their information from books. A further nineteen per cent obtained a lot of their information from parents, and eighteen per cent of them from television and films. An unfortunate twenty-nine per cent obtained only a little of their sex education from their parents. Obviously, sex education starts usually before adolescence and I would suggest that it needs to start as lightly and honestly as possible as soon as the child begins to enquire about it. The most helpful context is, I believe, the family.

At the end of the day, if our adolescents are going to experiment sexually (and it is unfortunately true that many of them will), then they will do so despite our most rigorous attempts to instil morality and to minimise opportunity. Opportunities will always be found, and externalised morality amounts to little more than religion anyway. The better way forward is for frank and honest discussion and the encouragement of a personal relationship with Jesus, to the extent that the clear directives in the Bible become understood and embraced from the heart, where they can be underscored by the witness of the Holy Spirit in the individual's conscience, and by the work of the Holy Spirit in his or her lifestyle. I would certainly want to make sure that the education I give to my children concerning sex and sexuality includes a full explanation of responsibility about contraception, so that should they choose to make decisions contrary to my own and the Bible's morality, they will at least be thinking responsibly concerning the consequences. To shy away from education and contraception on the grounds that it somehow encourages immorality, seems to me not only to be a logical non-sequitur, but dangerously irresponsible, particularly in an age of so many unwanted pregnancies and the transmission of so many sexual diseases, including the killer AIDS.

Doubtless there are many other areas we could have investigated, but with this not being a book on parenting, I wanted to restrict this chapter to a few hopefully useful practical tips. If what I have suggested is unworkable, or if there are more viable alternatives, I would be only too happy to hear from you.

In closing this chapter, it might be helpful to make you aware of the kind of advice I have given on areas similar to these to teenagers and adolescents themselves. It might therefore help you to obtain a copy of *The Teenage Survival Kit* and *The Teenage Revival Kit*, both published by Kingsway, where topics such as these and others are explored from the teenagers' perspective. You can then marry teaching aimed more at adults, teachers and youth leaders, to that which I have given to teenagers and adolescents, and measure the consistency between the two to find areas of helpful overlap.

CHAPTER ELEVEN

THE CHURCH OF TODAY

– YOUNG PEOPLE AND YOUR CHURCH

If church is to be a truly prophetic image of family, then it is vital that we allow our understanding of adolescence to permeate every aspect of the life of the church youth work. There is an established trend of decline in many UK churches which desperately needs to be reversed. The Anglican Church currently loses seventy-five per cent of its young people between the ages of thirteen to twenty, whilst the Roman Catholic and free churches lose fifty per cent. Sunday schools (or their equivalent) in those churches lose ninety-five per cent of all children over the age of fourteen years who do not come from a church family background. It is not enough to merely understand adolescence. The danger with a book like this is that we take on board the theory, but fail to understand the implications and implement the practice in our home or church lives. This chapter, then, is an attempt to give some headlines by way of a checklist for any parent, youth leader, or church youth group leader, to assess the effectiveness of his or her attempts to make integrated disciples through a church-based youth programme.

I want to suggest that there are five key elements which,

taken together and in the right order, stand a good chance of helping us develop good practice from good theory. These elements form a process, the end result of which is intended to be a well-integrated, fully-functioning, maturing young disciple of Christ in the life of the local church. The process quite logically begins with the participants.

Participants

The nature and content of what you do with your youth work in the local church setting will of course be determined by the nature of the young people for whom it is run. Fundamental questions must be asked. Are the young people mainly from Christian families within the church? Are they themselves Christians? Or, have they adopted the common attitude that they are Christians 'by default', that they are somehow God's 'grandchildren', who will therefore need to be made aware that God only has children, not grandchildren? If the participants are mainly Christian, this will necessarily affect the balance of the content of your programme. If they are mainly non-Christian, but from a Christian background, there will be areas of resentment and 'gospel-hardening' to be worked through. If, on the other hand, they are non-Christian from a non-church background, then obviously evangelism will be a higher priority for your youth work. So too will publicity and some form of active recruitment. Thus, further questions will be sparked by participants of this nature. Where are they to be found? What are their preferred recreational activities? Are there ways in which the church youth work can serve them in this? What is their perception of church? Of your church? Of God?

Thought will also need to be given at this stage to the specific age range that the youth work is attempting to cover. It will be worth bearing in mind the general age bands that adolescents fall into, as discussed in a previous chapter. It is certainly a mistake to try to make the youth work accomplish too much across too wide an age band. For this reason, I would recommend that the span of adolescence from ten to twenty-one is broken down as follows: ten to fourteen forms one peer group; fifteen to seventeen forms a second; and eighteen to twenty-one forms a third. There will always need to be flexibility within these age ranges, as you can have incredibly mature thirteen-year-olds, and extremely immature fifteen-year-olds. The point is not essentially their maturity levels, but in which group they feel most comfortable, whilst noting also the reaction of that group to the individual. An immature fifteen-year-old might want to be with his or her peer group in the fifteen- to seventeen-year-old age band, but may be found to be far too childish and disruptive and may better be integrated with the young children in the ten to fourteen age band. Observation, sensitivity and flexibility are the key words here.

It may seem very obvious to start our investigation of the place of youth within the church by looking at the nature of the participants in the youth group, but all too often churches set up programmes in an attempt to work with young people whom they feel they ought to be working with, rather than to work with those whom God has initially given. The whole point of a church-based youth work is that it should be user-orientated and user-friendly. Programmes that are merely imposed upon young people, without thought and reference to where they are at in background and age range, will at best produce attenders rather than participants, and at worst will cause young people to vote with their feet!

Purpose

Once the participants have been identified (which is a matter of either observing the youth you already have or hearing from God concerning the young people you might have in the future), the second part of the process in developing an integrated, discipling model of youth work within the life of your local church, is to ascertain the purpose of the youth group. The process must proceed in this order otherwise we are in danger once again of fitting people into – and making them serve – structures, rather than the other way around. The only exception to this order is where your church has no current youth work and no young people to be incorporated into one. If that is the case, then of course you become free under God to determine what the purpose of a church youth work will be before you start it up. It is relatively unlikely that you are suddenly going to be presented with a large number of converted young people, and therefore in this scenario it is highly likely that your purpose would be primarily evangelistic. However, that is by no means the only purpose for a church-based youth work, and I would like to suggest four complementary purposes, which we will identify one by one.

(a) Evangelism

If you are dealing with a group of young people who are as yet unconverted, either because they have no church background, or because they have resisted the efforts of their parents to see them converted, it will be necessary to make your primary purpose evangelism. Youth evangelism is a very fruitful field, but one fraught with potential for abuse, and consequently we will cover it in more detail in Chapter 13. It will be sufficient here to note that a youth work which is primarily evangelistic needs to be creative in its programming, attractive and relevant in its outreach, radical in its publicity and recruitment, and must essentially view evangelism in its broadest sense, incorporating social action projects and involvement in the local community by the young people themselves. The process of discipleship with young people frequently precedes conversion, and this needs to be borne in mind.

(b) Teaching

Even if evangelism is your primary purpose as a youth work, somewhere along the line (for the purposes of discipleship) you are going to have to consider teaching styles and content. Energy levels, concentration spans, idealism untempered with perspective, hatred of religion and hypocrisy – all of these will have their effect upon the style of your teaching. The need for experience, pressing issues of insecurity, peer group pressure, heightened sexual awareness – all of these will have impact upon the content of your teaching programme. My advice would be that your teaching programme should not only cover directly biblical issues, encouraging young people to understand the Bible, but also make sure that they are life-related, and as a minimum cover the issues raised in this book. The teaching would need to be broken down into short segments, to be visually orientated, to be experientially rooted in concrete and practical examples, to be accessible through the honesty and vulnerability of the teacher, and to involve active participation through projects, role play, interviews and discussion groups. And I would recommend it ought ideally to be approximately seventy per cent practical and thirty per cent theoretical/doctrinal.

(c) Friendship

The third aspect of the purpose of any growing and developing youth work ought to be the provision of friendship across the span of adolescence. I have used the word friendship deliberately in preference to fellowship, since many churches throw young people into an artificial climate of religion by generating corporate worship of God in an atmosphere of personal animosity amongst the young people themselves! It being impossible to love God and hate your brother (1 Jn), I would prefer to define this purpose as the building of realistic friendships, the exercising of the principles of Matthew 18, a deliberate defusing of conflicts, and the careful confrontation of relationship issues. Consequently, in the lives of many insecure and questioning adolescents this kind of lifeline of friendship can become a vital and valid one. Such friendships will be important to the gang mentality of the ten- to fourteen-year-olds, to the clique mentality of the fifteen- to seventeen-year-olds, and to the one-to-one relationships of the eighteen- to twenty-one-year-olds. It can become the primary forum within which behavioural patterns in relationships are worked out, and it is better by far that they are worked out in this context than merely at school or down at the local borough youth club!

It is valid and important that varieties of peer group defined by age do meet together throughout the church, and this certainly includes youth. Not only will peer groups learn quickest together, and not only will they evangelise best across their own peer group, but also of course friendships will be most healthily formed here. This is important to the health of the youth group and not least if situations of 'unequal yoking' (1 Cor 15:33, 2 Cor 6:14) are to be avoided.

(d) Pastoral

It will by now be readily observed that some means of pastoral care needs to be carefully implemented as we reach into the delicate lives of adolescents, and an outlet external to family life is helpful. This can best be found in a good and caring church-based youth group.

If I remember my Maths A-level correctly (since it's

many years ago now!) these four purposes can best be demonstrated in the form of a Venn diagram as below:

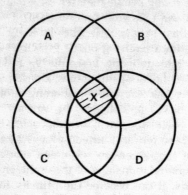

This is to say that none of the four purposes are mutually exclusive, and indeed in a well-balanced youth group (marked x in the diagram) all four will be in evidence. The danger, however, would be trying to cover all four in any one youth group meeting – that cannot be done. Each separate area needs a separate strategy, but all four strands should run parallel with one another, and there will of course be a degree of overlap.

Personnel

In an age of increasing specialisation in western society, and where the 'expert' carries the status almost of a guru, there has been a considerable emphasis in church life of finding one's personal calling, gifting and ministry. Since the word ministry rightly means works of service, I want to suggest that there are at least two spheres in all aspects of church life in which we serve.

The first sphere is the area of the general. This is where a job needs doing, and because we are all looking to out-serve one another, we don't wait around for God to reveal the answer as to whether it's our particular gifting or ministry before we set out the chairs, or put up the OHP screen!

The second area of service is the specific, where our particular gifts (natural gifts bestowed by the Father through creation; supernatural gifts bestowed by the Holy Spirit through his infilling; and ministry gifts bestowed by the Spirit of Jesus for the building of his church) are used and honed to serve others. I want to suggest that, just as God has a special place in his heart for young people (see Chapter 4), so too he has particular people whom he calls to work with them. In other words, being a church-based youth worker is an area for *specific* calling and gifting, rather than a *general* one.

It is a truism that need will always be greater than resources. It is also true that need does not constitute calling. In all aspects of church life we need to be men and women of God who are called of God, rather than driven by need (our own, or others). We have already seen in Chapter 3 that some youth workers are involved in youth work because they are driven to fulfil their own needs (such as for more security, self-worth, authority, kudos, role and recognition within the local body). I suggest that what is essential when we look at personnel in our five-point plan towards a healthy youth work is that we are looking for those who are called by God to work with youth. I have met too many youth workers who have been doing youth work for the last five years or more because the church 'needed' youth work and because there was no one else to fit the bill. In the long run such a youth worker will tend to be detrimental to the life of the youth work, since he or she will always reproduce whatever they are. If there is any resentment in their hearts concerning their vision for running a youth work, that will most surely communicate to youth people in all of their insecure sensitivities. It is far better if called personnel are not immediately apparent to actually pray them into place. This is not super-spiritual 'pie in the sky', but is a practical application of an exercise I have undertaken on a number of occasions by working my way through church membership address lists. It applies not only to youth workers, but also to evangelism team members, management and resource team members, school of prophecy team members, and so on.

When such personnel are in place (and it needs to be a team rather than one gifted individual), I would urge that they are given high recognition by their church, rather than low; that they are set aside by the church and prayed over, and that they are consistently and adequately supported. Support for church youth workers will take a variety of forms, but must as a minimum include: regular prayer cover; visits to the youth work by church members; additional personnel resources being made available as needed (eg, for pastoral or prayer support); regular prayer support through church prayer meetings and prayer partners; practical help (eg, where the youth leaders are spending one or more evenings working with the youth club – it may be that the home environment needs help by providing meals, doing housework, etc); financial resourcing for equipment and premises, and of course personnel themselves to be actively monitored and developed in order that they do not remain perpetual or inefficient youth leaders (eg, sending them to Brainstormers youth leaders training weekends, buying them all a copy of this book, etc!).

Programme

It is not possible in a book of this nature to dot all the 'i's' and cross all the 't's' concerning the implications of my observations on the development of adolescents. I ask the reader to forecast ahead from my observations to see what he or she thinks the practical outworking of such pressures and changes in the lives of an individual might mean for family life, or for the programme of the local church-based youth work. Sufficient here to say that the programme of any such youth work must take into account both the pressures and changes in the physical, emotional, mental, social and spiritual development of the adolescents. A few observations might be of help.

A brief glimpse at any of the teenage TV programmes (such as *DEF II* and *Reportage*) will indicate the prevalence of a magazine style approach to the programme format. This highlights the need for variety (bearing in mind that the difference between a grave and a rut is only 5'9"!), impetus and speed. It is worth remembering that the average attention span of a teenager is only ten to fifteen minutes long. Since we all learn by repetition, a good programme will be broken down into ten-minute slots, each slot making the same point, using a variety of media. Since teenagers are gregarious, it will also be interactive and will operate (as a microcosm of church itself) on at least four levels (the single individual, the cell, the congregational unit, and the celebration unit). A good youth programme should therefore seek to encourage individual development, small group development, have impact on the life of the local congregation, and also have an outlet across a wider-than-local church youth meeting (eg, in our own Pioneer Network of Churches through meetings such as 'Interface', which gather together between 100–200 young people from several churches).

Since energy and physical ability peak at seventeen to eighteen years old, it is important in the development of the adolescent that a good youth programme will also be pro-active in order to help the young people own the programme rather than have it imposed upon them, and it will involve the use of physical games and activities as well as projects. The fact that adolescents are learning to express conceptually their thoughts and feelings means that youth programmes must provide a forum for feedback. As many young people are brought up in an environment where most of their learning is made by visual observation, the youth programme ought to include visual aids and audio-visual aids. Christian teaching or gospel proclamation ought to be done thematically throughout the course of the entire programme, rather than episodically where too much reliance is placed upon an epilogue (and where creativity is restricted to shifting the epilogue into the middle to catch the young people out), such episodic proclamation will all too quickly produce a form of 'gospel hardening'. As adolescents are looking for what works, the programme should also be geared practically, rather than dealing with mere theoretical or theological abstracts. It should be based upon answering real questions, rather than supposed ones, and should go a long way to setting explained and reasonable parameters from God's perspective.

It might also be worth while noting that since any youth generation is currently approximately two years in generation, the programme itself should work to an approximate two-year cycle. Often youth works will take a slight dip at the end of two years because of this factor, which can be catered for through successful programming. Occasional special events placed at three- or four-monthly intervals, and at the end of the two-year cycle, can be strategic ways of combating the two-year blues! This is indicated by the hypothetical diagram below:

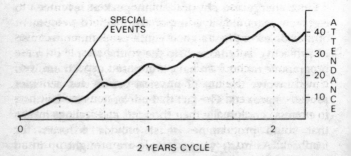

Premises

All too often care for premises has come before care for people, and I have known many cases where youth works which were successful were closed down because of damage caused to church premises (broken windows, let-off fire extinguishers, kicked doors, scuffed floors, etc).

You will have appreciated by now that this five-fold checklist has a flow of progression to it: existing *participants* for a youth work determine the *purpose* of that youth work. Where there are no existing participants, the purposes are first determined under God, and the participants are then recruited. The participants and the purpose for meeting together determine the need for called-out and prayed-in *personnel*, who then develop a *programme* suitable to the personnel (strengths and weaknesses), which will in turn facilitate the purpose of the group, which is to serve the participants. The programme will then to a degree determine the type or types of premises to be used. Thus, if the programme is mainly to be social action leading to evangelism amongst the unchurched, it might be necessary to hire local school premises, complete with playing fields, in order to best recruit those unchurched young people. If, on the other hand, the programme consists of imaginative Christian teaching to a small group of 'church family' young people, then it might be best to hold this in the front room of one of the church youth leaders. In any case, the order of the process is important, as premises and plant do not come before people.

I would put a plea for creativity in looking at premises and the way that they are decorated. Homes, short lease shop fronts, school halls, gymnasiums, sports centres, church halls, playing fields, marquees for summer projects, youth and community centres, non-alcoholic bars in previously closed pubs or indeed in family rooms in currently open pubs, are all possibilities. Whatever the venue suitable to the programme, personnel, purpose and participants, the premises must be made to work for you rather than against you. For example, a series of rooms which form a veritable rabbit warren will need a large amount of personnel simply to police the premises and make sure that illicit fire extinguisher release is kept to a minimum! This detracts from your ability to build relationships with the young people. If some form of 'ownership' can be established in premises then all the better – a mural painted on a wall, several copies of a logo lowered from the ceiling on ribbon banners, the use of background theme music, good and generally dark lighting, a good area for refreshments, the use of PA and discothèque systems where numbers warrant it, and setting up any focal point (eg, stage areas for presentation work) in the right place (ie, opposite the entrance and exit doors and away from the door to the toilets rather than next to them, in order to reduce distraction caused by wanderers), would all be helpful.

Integration

It has already been recognised in Chapter 1 that the Jewish society offered the emerging adolescent male the opportunity of stating to society, and to his culture in particular, that, 'I am now an adult' through the ritual of bar mitzvah at the age of thirteen. The youth came of age in his religious responsibilities and became fully a 'son of the commandment', which is the literal meaning of the phrase bar mitzvah.

During my work with British Youth for Christ (based for seven years in north-east London) I had the privilege and opportunity of working from time to time with Chris Chesterton of Nottingham Youth for Christ and of seeing his wife, Sheila, and their family together. Chris and Sheila instigated their own form of bar mitzvah within their family. At the age of thirteen, irrespective of gender, each of their children was the central figure in a major family celebration. At the same time, certain new responsibilities and privileges were made clear to the family as a whole:

- They were no longer regarded as children.
- Physical discipline was no longer an option.
- Flexibility regarding bedtimes and coming in was instituted.
- They were responsible for the consequences of their own actions.
- They were free to make their own choices about what they believed and about church life.
- They were expected to help around the house.
- They were led to expect consultation and not confrontation on family issues.

Whether or not you feel such a set process or ceremony is helpful in family or in church life, it is none-the-less true that those issues are being negotiated, usually between the ages of twelve to sixteen, in the life of the average adolescent in any case. There are certainly advantages in setting clear parameters and expectations upon this process. Lack of such parameters often produces the 'eternal youth group' complex, where the values of peer group friendship and activity, having once been perceived as advantageous, are adhered to beyond the age of adolescence. The result is that a peer group exists within the church that grows up together, relates together, and will eventually lose all its sense of purpose and focus because no clear parameters have been outlined as above in the 'bar mitzvah principle'.

There is nothing wrong whatsoever with a peer group remaining together for friendship, fellowship, evangelism, pastoral work and teaching, but if it stays together merely by default and through focusing in on what used to be, the result will be a gradual dissipation of purpose and then of participants. The better goal is clear parameters, defined expectations, a definite cut-off point and a successive format for that group to move into, and therefore a more realistic integration into wholistic church life. I would like to suggest that an essential part of integration is discipleship, since integration does not take place in a vacuum. The model for growth for young people is the same model which applies to us. It must involve example (Tit 2:6–8), opportunities for service, the giving away of responsibility, the possibility of decision making, opportunity to shape and direct plans which are being made (which impinge not only on the youth group, but upon the wider life of the church), and exposure to direct ministry and the prophetic word of God, as well as to theoretical teaching.

As we provide models for the successful discipleship and integration of young adolescents, it is important that we are providing female as well as male role models, to biblically and successfully disciple and integrate both sexes. Integration will also have an effect on our church culture, and we should therefore be aware of culture blocks, looking to *span* the generation gap rather than *close* it. The tastes of the adolescent generation are unlikely ever to equate with the tastes of young families, let alone OAPs, and to that extent the generation gap is a reality. But to see it as an enemy, where youth and older people are irreconcilable, would be inaccurate. Much of the style of music and presentation within our church meetings (and I include within this the newer churches of which I am a part) is dated and often provides a barrier for young people enjoying our meetings and contributing to them. I maintain that if God is perpetually doing a new thing, if it is true that we should be pioneers and not settlers, and if in any way additional grace and wisdom is given to those who are older and relatively more mature in the faith, then when it comes to the question of 'who moves' on worship and meeting styles, it ought to be *us* rather than the adolescents.

It might well be worth your while casting a positively critical eye over your church youth programme from the perspective of integration and discipleship. Even matters which seem small to us, may mean much to the identity-seeking adolescent. For example, do the adolescents appear in their own right in our church address lists, or are they merely incorporated under the name of their mothers and fathers? Do our young people get public profile in meetings (by which I mean more than a monthly family service or youth meeting)? Are they involved in helping serve alongside older people (thus avoiding the appearance of patronisation or exploitation) in setting out the chairs, the PA, the song sheets or hymn books? Do they have profile in conducting interviews with adults during the meeting? Are they represented in the worship group? Have they had involvement in the preaching timetable? In the prayer and ministry team?

The possibilities go on and on. Do the young people also have their own profile in church newsletters (more than a quiz at the bottom of the page for kiddies)? Are they represented on its editorial team? Would it be an idea to give them space on the church notice-board, which is not simply space for the youth group, but which is an integrated use of information which relates both to young and old alike?

The point of this chapter has been to provide you with a framework against which you can check the vision and direction of your church's youth programme. There should be enough here to spark your thinking and send you flicking back into previous chapters with a desire to apply some of the theories on understanding adolescence which we have looked at so far. But in reality this chapter only outlines the first phase of youth work – that is, the recognition that young people are not the church of tomorrow, but rather are the church of today. In order truly to reflect the heart of God, we need to move on from here and recognise that not only are young people the church of today, in many cases they are also the *leaders* of today and not just of tomorrow.

In the next chapter we will look at some practical steps forward in discipling, developing and releasing character and ministry amongst our young people in the context of church life.

CHAPTER TWELVE

NOT THE CHURCH OF TOMORROW

– DISCIPLING AND DEVELOPING YOUNG PEOPLE

The range of our possible sufferings is determined by the largeness and nobility of our aims. It is possible to evade a multitude of sorrows by the cultivation of an insignificant life. Indeed, if it be a man's ambition to avoid the troubles of life, the recipe is perfectly simple. Let him shed his ambitions in every direction, let him cut the wings of every soaring purpose, and let him assiduously cultivate a little life, with the fewest correspondencies and relations. By this means, a whole continent of afflictions and achievements will be escaped and will remain unknown.

From J.H. Jowett, *The Price of Enlargement*

Any person who is interested in the potential of a young life, who seeks to have something of the heartbeat of God for young people, and who would strive to present them perfect in Christ (Col 1:28), must be prepared to face the price of enlargement, both in his own life and in the life of the adolescents whom he seeks to serve. The difference between aspiration and achievement is development. It is important as we seek to integrate our young people into the life of our family and our church family through careful active discipleship that we are developing a commitment to be committed to development! That we are looking to deal with the important and not merely the urgent (can our teenager hear from God, or should he first stop smoking?), so that what we leave behind is gold rather than stubble (1 Cor 3:12).

It may be that the needs of your youth group seem complex and multiple. Or that the needs of each individual within it seem to be the same. Jesus had a consistent pattern for dealing with multiple need. We see him demonstrate it in Matthew 4:23–5:2, again in Matthew 9:35–10:5, and then in Matthew 28:18–20. When faced with the multitudes, with their problems and with urgent need on each of these three occasions, Jesus turns away from the problem and the multiple need and turns towards the disciples. The principle here is one of sowing and reaping. It is a matter of multiplication. What you impart into the life of the one, you will reap in the lives of the many. It is what lay behind the statement of John Wesley: 'Give me one hundred men on fire for God, and I will turn the nation around.' It is why Billy Graham said that if he had his time over again, he would take groups of people and train and impart to them what God had given to him. It is the principle that if needs are to be met, then resources must be multiplied. Parable after parable in Scripture deals with multiplication – which is the essential growth principle of the kingdom of God – rather than addition. Development and discipling of adolescents will not only serve to integrate them better into church life, but will also better equip them to be the church of today. This is after all our ultimate purpose.

Selection

The first step to this type of discipleship is selection. Jesus practised this in Matthew 4:18, and we need to understand very clearly that God has no problem with dealing with

154

the unsaved youth who at the moment our churches are not touching. He has no problem with the harvest. Nor does God have any problem with preparing workers; God's problem rather lies with getting his hands on suitable workers.

Yet in all this God has always chosen people who in the world's eyes would seem to be failures. Jesus' original team of twelve included two brothers who quarrelled so much that they earned themselves the nickname of Sons of Thunder. It included Peter, rampantly insecure and constantly going over the top, whether it be his assertion that he would never betray Jesus shortly before he did so three times, whether it be his leaping out of a boat only to sink when he took his eyes off Jesus, or whether it be his declared intent to build not one temple to the only true living God, but three to Jesus, Elijah and Moses! Or perhaps his plea for Jesus to wash him all over when in fact his feet would suffice! The team also included Matthew who was a tax collector and would be unwelcome on most teams! It included Thomas, who despite the *one* unfortunate incident, earned himself forever after the nickname 'doubting Thomas'. And, of course, Jesus' team included the only named position (that of treasurer), which went to the one man on the team who proved himself capable, not only of stealing the money designated for the poor, but ultimately betraying Jesus – Judas Iscariot!

God has always chosen the ordinary of this world in order to confound the wise; consequently, people tend to give God the glory, rather than other people. And so, Peter and John in Acts 4:13 are called literally ungrammatical idiots, but the big difference, of course, is that they had been with Jesus.

The lesson for us here is twofold. Firstly, we do need to select people for our programme of discipleship and integration, recognising that not everybody is at the same place in their commitment or their walk with God. And secondly, we need to recognise that sometimes the people

God chooses are not the people whom we would naturally choose, and that very often those who seem to be furthest away from the kingdom are in fact the closest to it. If you yourself are involved in the discipleship and integration of young people into family or church life, then let me suggest a few hot tips when it comes to the process of selection.

Firstly, make your selection of whom to disciple (or if you are dealing with only one individual, what one area of their life needs to be tackled first) only after Holy Spirit-led prayer and fasting.

Secondly, remember that because people are at different stages of their development and commitment to Jesus it is permissible to work at different levels with different groups of disciples, just as Jesus did. So Jesus had his one-to-one relationship with the disciple whom he loved the most (Jn 21:22). He related to Peter, James and John more closely than to the rest (Mk 9:2). Then he had the twelve disciples (Lk 9), followed by the seventy or seventy-two (Lk 10). And there are additional references in Scripture to disciples in a wider circle of 120, 500, and 4 or 5,000.

Thirdly, it really is important that we get God's perspective on the people whom we select, otherwise we may be in danger of 'people blindness'. Jesse could be accused of people blindness when he disregarded his youngest son, David, who was selected and anointed by the prophet Samuel as king of Israel, replacing Saul in 1 Samuel 16:6–13. This is often where we need outside help and perspective from other church youth group leaders or from the church leadership itself, and this is certainly true in our family where it is particularly easy to get locked into faults and failings from the past. People blindness tends to keep us remembering people the way they were, or for their faults rather than their potential. Of course, the converse is also true: we don't always want to be working with those people who present the greatest challenge and seem to be the most recalcitrant – Jesus spent time with

Peter, James and John as well as with Judas! It is important to remember that we must always be prepared to lose people, as not everyone will want to be discipled in Christ and integrated into his church.

Fourthly, we are looking for people who are teachable and available, for people who will demonstrate a servant heart and who have a measure of faithfulness and loyalty. Since a disciple is ultimately a learner, a follower and one who keeps a discipline, we are not simply looking for ability, so much as for availability to change. All adolescents will have their problems (as will all adults!), but the issue is not whether they have a problem, but what they will do with that problem. Similarly, if you are dealing with an area in the life of your adolescent son or daughter, look for that area to work on first where there is already a measure of acceptance and teachability.

Fifthly, in all of this beware of setting too high a standard. It is important to note that as church leadership teams (including church youth group leadership teams) get older and more experienced, so the qualifications get higher and the standard expected of ministry becomes more strenuous. This means that we need to be taking action if we are going to make space for new and emerging young leaders, and we must constantly be asking ourselves the question, 'Can they do now in God what we did then for him?'

Demonstration

Having selected the key individuals who will be breakthrough people and leaders within their own peer group, or having selected the one or two areas in the life of the adolescent for whom you are responsible, it is important next to demonstrate the kind of lifestyle which you wish to see imparted and instructed into the life of that individual or group. Jesus lived this out himself in Matthew 4:23. It was Albert Schweizer who said that, 'Example is not the best means of leadership, it is the only means'. It was Jesus who lived it out.

In your demonstration of principles, it is important always to remind the individual adolescents (particularly at their stage of emotional vulnerability and insecurity) that their identity comes before their function – ie, you accept them for who they are, rather than what they do. This can never be more true than when they become Christians; Jesus accepted them as they are for who they are, not what they have or haven't done, and it is our job to represent Christ to them. Demonstration revolves largely around finding areas to serve the individuals, and this will be good for the humility levels of any parent or youth leader. It will be remembered that service works in both the general and the specific, but the principle remains the same: that we look to outserve one another having the same attitude (Greek, *phroneo*, meaning 'think, feel, do') that Christ had in Philippians 2:5.

So, if we want our youth group to be involved in the setting out of chairs, we must make sure that *we* are involved in the setting out of chairs. If we want our youth group to understand the importance of moderation in alcoholic consumption, we must make sure that we are setting a good example in this by extolling the positives of controlled social drinking in a realistic environment (this may necessitate a trip to the pub!), along with stressing the negatives of alcohol abuse. If we want to impart into the understanding of our adolescent son the need to be in at a certain time when requested, it will be important that we too are demonstrably thoughtful and punctual in our use of time in relation to the rest of the family. It is always worth remembering when it comes to this point of demonstration that those whom we lead and serve will always attach importance to that to which we give priority. Stressing punctuality and always being late will not wash in the life of any adolescent.

Instruction

The primary purpose of biblical instruction is character formation, not gift acquisition. Therefore biblical instruction promotes intrinsic and not extrinsic development, imparting skills and not merely giving answers. Such instruction will be aimed at the heart and the head in accordance with Proverbs 29:18 and Hosea 4:6, on the basis that information alone will only lead the adolescent into frustration, but revelation with information will lead him or her into transformation. A self-critical assessment of the way that you relate to your adolescent child or youth group can helpfully start by asking the question: 'Do you use people, or do you cultivate them?' and, 'Do you direct them, or do you develop them?'

The right kind of biblical instruction will necessitate a careful use of your time along the lines of Jesus' time management with his disciples. All the elements of everyday living were used by Jesus (often visually or allegorically) in order to teach and instruct. In Mark 3:14 it's clear that Jesus had the disciples with him, and I would always urge a creative use of time between father and child, or youth leader and youth group members (making sure, of course, that you avoid opposite sex complications and one-to-one lock-up.

In Matthew 18:1–4 we can see that Jesus encouraged the questions of his disciples, but was always able to answer their heart, rather than simply their questions. As it is often the case that the question from an adolescent is not the real issue – because of limited communication skills or because of complicating factors such as role play, fear or insecurity – it is important that we seek God's wisdom and discernment to enable us to do what Jesus did and find the heart of the matter.

In Matthew 19:14 we also find Jesus rebuking his disciples in love because there was no fear of rejection; Jesus was not scared of losing the disciples, and the disciples were not scared that Jesus would abandon them. This issue of acceptance and affirmation is an important one in biblical instruction. The model which Jesus used to instruct involved pre-training, followed by training (which consisted of actually doing), followed by feedback or 'unpacking', followed by the disciples doing the work on their own (a cycle clearly seen from Mark 10 and 17).

In order to facilitate this kind of instruction it is important to think strategically concerning your programming of a youth work, your use of local and translocal ministries, your blend of training and doing (I would suggest fifty-fifty), of practical and theoretical (seventy-thirty), your mix of evangelism and pastoral (again fifty-fifty), and your strategic use of books, tapes and conferences.

Impartation

In Matthew 10, where there is a commissioning of the disciples to work in a team, there is also a clear impartation from Jesus to the disciples which goes beyond the level of mere instruction: there is a catching (albeit imperfect!) of Jesus' heart and burden. In the Old Testament, in Exodus and Leviticus, the high priest would go into the presence of God carrying, metaphorically, the people of God on his head and shoulders in the form of twelve semi-precious stones arranged around his garments, representing the twelve tribes of Israel. In becoming our great High Priest (Heb 4:14), Jesus himself carries this same burden, and if you wish to impart all of God that you have, you must in turn learn how to carry the people of God (including young people for whom he has a special place in his heart) into his presence. This will involve you in prayer for, and prayer with, those young people wherever possible.

It is a spiritual fact of life that you will always reproduce yourself, a fact perhaps never more scary than when observed by a parent in the life of their developing child. It is therefore important that in the process of impartation we recognise our own strengths and weaknesses, and therefore key in to the benefits of team work wherein weaknesses can be compensated for, and where one-to-one lock-up can be avoided. Expression of appreciation and affirmation will always be a key part of impartation, as will the pain of allowing our protégés (be they our children or our youth group) to pay the price of failure in order to cope later with the price of success. Young people are followers, and impartation is part of a process which decides simply whom and what they will follow. Impartation is about all that which is best caught rather than taught.

Delegation

In Matthew 28:16–20 we see the ultimate example of delegation when Jesus delegates the Great Commission to his disciples. An essential part of developing, releasing and integrating young people into the life of the family and the church family is the giving of decision-making power to them. Of course, we always retain the right to question decisions, but it is usually better that decisions are taken than that none are made at all. Delegation works well in an atmosphere of trust, because trust stimulates security, whereas mistrust stimulates stagnation and fear. There will, of course, always be a price to pay here since, as John Wimber points out, trust is usually spelled R-I-S-K! However, it is important that we provide a safe environment for delegation to be effectively practised, since mistakes are not sin, and the worst that can possibly happen as an adolescent moves forward in an attempt to grasp responsibility and action a project is . . . ultimate disaster!

I want to suggest that this is not as bad as breeding a generation of young people suffering from kakahaphicphobia – the fear of making mistakes. It is important that as responsibilities are being taken up for the first time, when adolescents are spreading their wings (either emotionally, spiritually, physically, socially or mentally), failure is seen as a positive learning experience which has all the potential of being redemptive. Working with adolescents is not about changing metaphorical nappies and wiping allegorical noses! It is not about 'Keep your noses clean and keep your mouths shut'! It is not about learning to live safe, defensive Christian lives, but rather learning to live unsafe, offensive (to God's enemies) lives! In this context, failure can become a doorway to maturity instead of a trap-door to obscurity.

Of course, the danger for us as disciplers is that the failure of our disciples often reflects on us, and our tendency therefore is to seek to curb them. It is easier to drop someone once they have failed you, than to get them to do things right! We would perhaps do well to remember that when delegation is involved, those on the job usually have the best ideas, on the basis that where God calls he also equips.

When something goes well, it is therefore important that credit and recognition are given as this is also a part of successful delegation. Nor does delegation simply mean giving up the bad jobs or the ones that you'd like to let go of – it also entails giving up the good jobs. This in turn will challenge our own insecurities and self-worth, which is usually a useful exercise!

Youth church

It seems to me that by adopting some of the principles outlined in this and other chapters we can overcome the danger of non-integration of young people into our churches. Given that much ground has already been lost, this will of course necessitate a strategy of evangelism which we will look at in the final chapter of this book.

However, there is one other possible alternative which has gained considerable ground in recent years, which seeks to develop and disciple young people without integrating them into existing churches. This model is found in the formation of 'youth churches'. The concept recognises the real needs of young people coming from a different worldview and culture, having met with a real and radical conversion experience of Christ but finding it difficult to integrate into the worldview and culture of the average church. There have been various attempts at establishing youth church where the focus has been specifically on reaching young people and then developing them in God in a culture and environment most suitable to them. In some cases youth church seems to have evolved rather than being specifically planned for, but the concept is taking hold and a number of established denominational churches are now seeking alternative services or meetings with a specific youth flavour. Examples exist in Sheffield, Swindon, Woodford Green, Southampton, Leeds and a number of other places as well. Sometimes these youth churches have grown up under the auspices of a number of local churches working together with or without the help of inter-denominational para-church organisations like BYFC, or Heartbeat's New Generation Ministries.

The strengths of youth church are obvious in that they tend to be more culturally relevant to young people. There may be more room for the development of young leaders within this context, and it makes integration into this particular form of church easier for new converts from the same peer grouping. However, the weaknesses of youth church are equally obvious. Pragmatically, there are difficulties with the passing of time; would we need to keep starting youth churches for each generation, and if so what constitutes a generation? If it is true that a youth generation in this country is approximately two years, do we need to start a new youth church every two years? Or could a youth church span more than one youth generation?

My observation is that no youth church in existence at the moment has been able to span more than an absolute maximum of four such two-year youth generations, and they realistically work better at either the top or bottom end of this span, ie, from sixteen to twenty years or from twenty to twenty-four years. It is also true that existing churches automatically miss out on the life, challenge and vitality that young people bring if all of those young people are segregated into one specific church. Nor would such a church be a full expression of church life (in a similar way that a black or a white church is not a full expression of church) given that practically and theologically church is meant to be a prophetic statement of the reconciliation of polarities as an inherent part of the gospel (Rom 10:12, Gal 3:28, Col 3:11). There then occurs a serious lack of localised community expression of what church life is all about, namely the family of God learning to live in harmony and peace with one another and with society despite differences of age, class, gender and position. Youth church has a further serious weakness of not providing role models from young to old, or indeed from old to young. This in turn will tend to entrench both sets, old and young, in stereotypical ideas concerning their opposites. There also exists the very real question of how such youth churches are to be resourced, and by whom? What are the points of accessibility, communication and accountability?

My own feeling on youth church is that there ought to be no such animal! We have, however, recognised a need for peer group relationships within the overall body of the church, and it seems to me that a good way forward is to establish youth cells or congregations which are clearly a part of (and function together with) the overall church, but might have their own individual meetings, programmes, styles, and so on. On this basis I would equally argue for the validity of an elder congregation, or an Asian congregation, or an Afro-Caribbean congregation, providing they are committed to, accountable to, and accessible to an overall (wider) church in leadership, heart, vision and resource.

We have looked previously at young people as the

church of today. Much has been written that could readily be accused of idealism, and indeed it is true that we as a church have lost much ground in serving the youth generation of this nation. The vast majority of the 8.25 million young people in the UK are as yet unreached with the gospel of Jesus Christ, and are not in a state of active rejection of or rebellion from it. I can only plead that the principles I have outlined in previous chapters are workable and are based on my experience of church-based youth work over the course of the last fourteen years.

I would like to close this chapter with a few verbatim quotations from young people whom I have worked with over the years, to indicate what a privilege, joy and a constant thrill it is to see some of these principles put into practice, and to see God do what only he can in the lives of the people for whom his heart burns:

'I have God as my best friend and I love the Lord.'

'The most exciting things that happened to me this week were: I became a Christian on Saturday night, I was filled with the Holy Spirit on Wednesday, I now know Jesus as a friend and Father. PS. I prayed for a girl who had asthma and she was cured and it really made me believe even more that God is great.'

'God has made me into a Christian; this is the best thing that has ever happened in my life.'

'I had a sort of demon from Satan which was stopping the Holy Spirit getting through, but we prayed and now I am free from it and God has come into my life – praise the Lord.'

'God has said a lot to me – I was filled with the Spirit and went stone cold out and hit the wall (!). I was prayed with because as my parents are divorced, I felt that I had no physical father. This week God has shown me that he can be a physical and spiritual Father. In this way I was healed emotionally and now feel a lot more confident in myself.'

'I have learnt that I shouldn't be ashamed of being a

Christian, and also it doesn't look stupid dancing and raising your hands. I have really felt the Holy Spirit, and being with a group of Christians all praying was great.'

'I really got to know God. I also got really close to my friends. I realise that I didn't know God before and now I do.'

'I was healed of my thumb infection which I have had for three years, and which the doctors and nurses could do nothing about.'

'God made me as I am and I should love myself because I am the best person I can be. I should not doubt God's voice. I have learnt to reach out to God when he calls me and not hold back.'

'I have come to know God as a real friend. He has always been a father before, but not a friend. Also, I have seen my friend become re-filled with the Holy Spirit.'

'God showed me how much he loves me. And that he wants to be my friend. And he wants to talk with me about anything. He has also shown me that he loves me no matter what.'

'God has healed my throat. On Saturday I could not speak or praise the Lord because there was like a lump in my throat. I was prayed for and now I can praise as loud as I like – which is very loud! Also, I feel closer to God and my family.'

'God has brought me out of the darkness, because I was very shy, but now I am not. I was lost, but now I am closer to God.'

Good stuff, eh? Worth working for!

CHAPTER THIRTEEN

GO GET 'EM!

– YOUTH EVANGELISM AND REVIVAL

With the majority of the world's population now officially classified as youth, it will come perhaps as no surprise that a majority of the approximately 120,000 people who die every day (that's more than one per second, each second of every day) are going to be youth. Not only because of the population ratio, but also because of the particular peculiarities and stresses (external and internal) that adolescence brings. It should also come as no surprise at this stage in the book, that a majority of the three million or so unemployed in the UK are young. Or that a majority of the approximately four million drug abusers in the UK are young, with the average age for offences involving drug abuse being fifteen. And it will come as no surprise that the majority of the 170,000-plus abortions that take place on a yearly basis in the UK are carried out on *young* girls. And that, of course, the majority of victims of sexual abuse in the UK are young people, a startling example of which is that London is the male prostitute centre of Europe.

This same category, youth, is exhibiting an increasing upsurge of interest in things which the Bible specifically describes as the occult, forbidden, hidden, or that which is detestable and an abomination to God. There are many such references in Scripture, and it might be helpful to outline a few of them here: Ex 7:11–12; 22:18; Lv 19:26, 31; 20:6–27; 1 Sa 15:23; 28:3; 2 Ki 21:5–6; 2 Ch 33:6; Is 2:6; 8:19; Je 27:9–10; Zc 10:2; Mal 3:5; Acts 8:9 following; Acts 16:16 following; Acts 19:19; Gal 5:19–21; 1 Tim 4:1; and 2 Tim 3:8.

And so, although between seventy-six and eighty-two per cent of young people in the UK believe in God, in the East London schools in which I taught between 1978 and 1985, approximately fifty per cent of those in the classes that I saw had attended a séance, and up to eighty per cent of them had practised with tarot cards and ouija boards, some of them within the confines of their RE lessons in schools! National statistics indicate that somewhere around sixty per cent of teenagers consult their horoscope on at least a weekly basis.

And yet, whatever we are to make of the various prophetic words which have been spoken over the UK in recent months and years (and which I personally want to align myself with), often from accredited prophetic ministries (including Rodney Kingstone, Gerald Coates and Martin Scott), there seems little doubt that God has been speaking clearly and consistently concerning revival in the UK. A revival which will affect not only our nation, but the rest of Europe and the nations beyond, once again through the sending of missionaries; and a revival which sees much of its impact first upon, secondly through, and then thirdly into the youth generation, not only of our churches, but also of our unchurched. It is churches which get revived, and nations/people groups which get resurrected!

There have been a number of such significant prophetic words linking God visiting these islands with revival and using youth and impacting youth. If we as a church are to learn to take such words seriously we must begin to prepare for the outworking of God's Holy Spirit, which biblically was always prophesied with a particular emphasis on youth (Joel 2:28–29, Acts 2:17–21). It would certainly be very much in keeping with God's revealed character in Scripture, where we have already seen in Chapter 4 that God has in the past been at pains to skip the faithless generations to reach a whole new generation of younger people, in order to get his will done.

It is statistically true that the optimum age for conversion in western society still remains at fourteen years and nine months. This, alongside the increasing statistics of those youth who are most at risk in our society, and the positive input of God's prophetic word concerning who (youth) and how (youth) he wishes to move, should combine our faith and practice to focus on evangelising our current youth generation as thoroughly and effectively as possible, bearing in mind all the lessons we have learned in this book so far.

In many ways this chapter is a summary, with a particular focus (evangelism), of what has been said in the rest of the book. It is an attempt to help you cross the 't's' and dot the 'i's', drawing out the implications of what we have learned together thus far. Perhaps a few helpful general observations need to be made, followed by some specific recommendations for youth evangelism.

Parental control

It should be noted that the teenager is neither legally, morally, socially, emotionally, physically, nor mentally in complete control of his or her life and destiny. There are many impinging and influencing factors, laws, restrictions and authority figures which hedge the adolescent round for better or worse, providing a bewildering variety of internal and external pressures. Consequently, any commitment which an adolescent makes, be it to CND, U2's fan club, the local youth club, or indeed to God himself, can only be a commitment for which the adolescent is in control. The heart commitment may be 110 per cent, but youth evangelism must always take account of factors which, by their pragmatic outworking, may appear to reduce the effectiveness of that commitment. Thus a teenager desiring to go on with God may make a commitment to God, but still only be allowed to attend youth group mid-week and not church on a Sunday, because his parents are 'anti-religion', or are concerned about cults or fanaticism. Such factors inhibiting the outworking of whole-hearted commitment are of course not always negative, but rather are sometimes simply facts of life. Certainly, legally and for wisdom's sake such factors must be adhered to and respected by youth workers and youth leaders.

The process of redemption

It then becomes a healthy and positive challenge to realise that increased autonomy and responsibility in the life of the teenager should always have a direct implication for increased levels of commitment to God. The commitment may be absolute, but its outworking will be dynamic and flexible, not static. There is then a very real sense that youth evangelism depends not so much on crisis decisions, but upon a mature and reflective, progressive outworking of such decisions. The reality of this proposition is best demonstrated by the disastrous consequences of numbers of teenagers growing up into their late teens and early twenties, who seek to live a Christian life off the basis of a Sunday School commitment. When the former youthful commitment has not been actively encouraged and developed to reflect the state of the latter older more autonomous lifestyle, then we end up with stunted and immature Christian birth, and with large areas of lifestyle not submitted to the lordship of Christ.

Of course, every change in the life of a believer brings about the need for re-evaluation of commitment and submission to the lordship of Christ, but this is never going to be more true than in the lives of adolescents, for whom change is happening at a quicker pace and in every life-related area, as seen in the early chapters of this book. I remain convinced that this is one of the reasons why many very real decisions for Christ never mature into real disciples for him, with the adolescent growing through into adulthood in every area except for his or her spiritual development. This is, at least in part, a shortfall of the discipleship programmes of our churches, rather than an indictment upon youth evangelism. There can be little doubt that on many occasions a very real inward regeneration takes place in the life of an adolescent making an initial commitment to Christ. But this will none the less take a considerable amount of time to work its way through into an outward appearance of conversion in the life of that individual. Psychological, mental, emotional, relational, social and moral adjustments must be made in the lives of adolescents who, in all of these areas, are in such turmoil, if their initial commitment to Christ is to take root in all of these other areas of their lives as well as in the spiritual.

Whatever the cause of their commitment (which may have been made on the basis of repentance of sin, or the need for God as a Father, a friend or a forgiver, or because of the need for the assurance of their future, or whatever – all perfectly valid) it will certainly not be an overnight achievement, even if literal conversion is. The verbs most commonly used for salvation in the New Testament come from the Greek word *soteria*, which is a kind of Greek equivalent of the Hebrew word *shalom*, meaning peace, wholeness, prosperity and restored relationship with God. The Greek word carries connotations of forgiveness, healing and wholeness, and is often written in the present continuous tense, carrying the literal implication of: 'I have been saved; I am being saved; I will be saved'. Salvation in the New Testament has always been written of, and seen and understood by the church, as a process. Obviously, all processes have a starting point, and every process will under God have a finishing point, and between the start and the finish we have the assurance that Jesus is both the author and perfecter of our faith (Heb 12:2), and consequently we are being changed from glory into glory (2 Cor 3:18). But in the meantime, the working out of salvation and the processes of sanctification are going on throughout the lifetime of the believer.

This stress on the process, which must be an inherent part of our understanding of youth evangelism, will help us avoid short-term disappointment when professions of faith do not automatically turn into committed disciples. There is no such guarantee with professions of faith made by adults, who in many ways have lives and lifestyles which are much more stable and autonomous than those of adolescents. We therefore should not expect it of their juniors. Seeing youth evangelism as part of a process of decision and outworking, where discipleship goes hand in hand with evangelism (which, biblically, it always should anyway – see the Great Commission in Matthew 28:16–20), will stop us from playing the numbers game. It will help us to resist the temptations of boosting our own self-worth and self-security by counting success as the number of those professing faith, (the 'numbers game'), and will keep a proper sense of perspective, helping us to avoid the dangers of disappointment and resentment when those into whom we are pouring our life and faith apparently fail to respond to Christ. It will also help us to understand that in a very real way it is impossible to fail in evangelism, since God's word will always accomplish that for which it was sent (Is 55:11).

The Engels' Scale, which perceives people as being on a sliding scale of proximity to God, some nearer, some further away, can be seen never to be truer than with the adolescent, for whom proximity to God requires a number of sliding scales – probably at least one for every changing life-related area! How close to God is the adolescent in the realm of the emotions, the thought processes, the physical, the social? Such an understanding of youth evangelism, and the process it involves, will also underline once again for us the vital part which discipleship and teaching takes in all youth evangelism. Often with young people, discipleship precedes conversion.

Decisions provoked, disciples produced

However, emphasis on the process is *not* intended to take away or detract from the biblical need for 'crisis' decisions. The Bible makes very clear the need for some form of decisive and usually public commitment to Christ (Rom 10:9, Mt 10:32–33). Such decisions are clear-cut, provide a helpful anchor point in the shifting turmoil of changing emotions in the life of an adolescent, are a response of obedience to God and therefore will be honoured by him, and they give a helpful handle for those seeking to help the adolescent in his or her commitment, as a point of referral. Providing that such crisis decisions allow for later fluctuation and possible failure, and they are placed in the context of the beginning of a process, I would *urge* that youth evangelism be a culmination *both* of the decision provoked, *and* the disciple produced.

Jesus certainly seems to have operated the same way himself with his own disciples – and it is difficult to state whether he was discipling them or evangelising them. None-the-less, his communication process, which involved the sharing of lifestyle with an extended period of relatively low-key communication, did have a variety of highlights or 'crisis' decisions where particular questions or situations were posited of the disciples, and a reaction was requested (Mt 16:13–20, 17:1–13, 19:16–22).

Practical evangelism

And so to some practical considerations in the area of youth evangelism. How does it best take place?

Firstly, you need to target your people group (Jesus told us to go and make disciples of all people groups/nations – Mt 28:16–20), bearing in mind that your people group should be decided by activity, geography, demography and age. Are you therefore targeting primarily eleven- to fourteen-year-olds, fifteen- to eighteen-year-olds, eighteen- to twenty-one-year-olds (age)? Do they share a particular background in common – are they, for example, from a middle-class housing estate or a local council estate (demography)? Are they all members of a local gang or youth club? Do they have a particular interest in common, eg, football or snooker (activity)? Do you wish to further your definition and targeting by concentrating on one particular school, or on three or four schools from a common catchment area? Is there instead perhaps a particular adolescent subculture that you wish to aim at, eg, goths, casuals, soul boys, rave or party-goers? Or perhaps you've noticed that there's a large group of young people who meet on an informal, but frequent basis, around certain key features of your local shopping estate, such as the doner kebab van, the local pub, the car park of the local ten pin bowling alley, the video shop or the local rec? Perhaps the summer months, when school is out, could provide you with a week's scheme to train young people in American football, which the setting up of a marquee with live music in the evenings might help promote. Or maybe you will start with what you already have, a large number of semi-churched young teenagers, whose commitment to God is nebulous, as they seem to feel that they are his 'grandchildren' by dint of their committed Christian parents! Or perhaps for you it's a thriving but relatively unchurched uniformed organisation attached to your denomination. In any case, some serious definition of *whom* you are seeking to reach, then *why* and *how*, needs to be done. You will need clear *goals* (which are measurable, attainable, specific and time orientated), all *written down* and *owned* by the leadership *team*.

Other books have seen it as their brief to write in more detail on how evangelistic events can best be planned, and I would recommend that you look at British Youth for Christ's *This Generation* Youth File, and also Steve Chalke's very practical *The Christian Youth Manual* (Kingsway Publications: Eastbourne, 1992).

It will be sufficient in the closing parts of this chapter for me simply to note that any programme of evangelism amongst young people should include at least some of the following constituent parts:

1. Schools work

Any youth communicator worth his salt needs to be acquiring training on the provisions of the 1944 and 1988 Education Acts, which stipulate non-proselytisation of young people, but require mandatory religious education through the school curriculum. The emphasis that the 1988 Education Reform Act places on this means that in many cases schools are crying out for external, good quality input into their RE/Personal and Social Education/Moral Studies syllabus, and also for input into assemblies which are required by law to take place on a daily basis.

Training in schools work is another subject in itself. But youth workers able to understand young people and communicate with them, need not necessarily be in fear of this avenue of opportunity where, without abuse of privilege and without preaching (either in style or content), they can communicate useful, practical, moral, irreligious, biblical truth to large numbers of young people. In so doing, they can build for themselves the first step of a platform of multiple contact (whereby they see young people in schools, on the streets, in the youth clubs and in their youth club) around their community. Headmasters are particularly keen on this word 'community', and the positive (not merely critical) input of Christians from local churches on PTAs and school governorships, where parents are sending their children to these very schools, means that there should be plenty of opportunity for linking local church to local school as an endeavour to build this bridge between school and community.

BYFC, who have a long history of very effective schools work, have produced a number of helpful aids to getting started, including their schools workers pack – anyone interested would be well advised to contact them, as well as Interschools Christian Fellowship (addresses at the back of this book). Ultimately, however, the best training is doing, and this can be embarked upon by the interested youth workers placing themselves alongside an accredited and experienced schools worker for about a week in order to pick up the basics.

2. Christian Union work

Ultimately, the best means of evangelism is peer group to peer group evangelism, whereby the evangelists are indigenous to their own group. Evangelism, therefore, works best across homogenous units (although this is a means of evangelism, not a picture of the church, which is best represented across heterogenous units – see the discussion earlier in Chapter 12 on youth church). Consequently, attention should be given by any self-respecting youth worker to building up and encouraging the work of the Christian Unions within the schools. They are the peer group on the job!

Christian Unions can be notoriously lacking in drive, energy, credibility and direction, but all of these things can be rectified, often with external help. Providing a list of good visiting speakers to the leaders of Christian Unions is helpful. So is providing prayer support from your local church, and finances where necessary for publicity and evangelistic activity. So is teaching on basic discipleship subjects (eg, Bible study, prayer, worship, Holy Spirit, self-worth, evangelism, and so on, as well as practical training on topics such as how to take an assembly effectively. Any Christian Union should be encouraged to have at least a three-fold purpose of evangelism/ teaching/ friendship. If a youth worker is working across a number of schools, he or she will find it possible to link Christian Unions in occasional inter-school events. This will give a sense of larger identity and will encourage Christian Unions to be outward-looking in praying for the needs of others, as well as encourage a sharing of resources and the opportunity for inter-church Christian Union evangelistic events (eg, concerts, sports days, barbecues and discos).

3. Special events

These obviously cannot be done in a vacuum and therefore thought must be given to *where* and *how* they will be publicised, and *whom* they are aimed at. None the less, there is a lot of room for creative specialist events which will draw a large youth audience. These can be publicised by leaflet drops through detached youth work, through local schools work, through local youth clubs, through the local press, through the careers office, and of course through your own church youth groups. Special events need much forward planning and professional approach in terms of content and publicity, and a creativity stimulated by an understanding of adolescence, perhaps as outlined by this book! They can include youth concerts, adventure weekends, lock-ins, lock-outs, discos, raves, debates, sports events, healing meetings, workshops connected to drama or motor-bikes, and so on.

4. Major missions

It needs to be borne in mind that whenever churches plan a major mission, very often the main impact, even if not specifically targeted, will be amongst young people. In the 1980s a series of major missions around England and to London found this to be the case. For example at *Mission England* with Billy Graham, fifty-four per cent of people who responded were under the age of eighteen! This is not a bad thing, but it does mean that such major missions should be taking more seriously the impact upon youth and planning events and nurture accordingly, both at the mission and local church events level.

5. Targeting specific peer groups

If for whatever reason you find that a young person or young people get saved from a particular peer group, (as happened with our church's Chichester-South Congregation among the goths), the situation should promote the question, 'Is God giving us this particular people group at this particular time?' If so, then support needs to be put alongside those new Christians within that group, as they will be the most effective in reaching their peers. There also needs to be some representation of that peer group on the youth leadership team, or someone who has a particular vision and heart in that direction. In our own church this happened when a guy called Greg Valerio, himself saved from a background of drugs and the occult, proved to have a very effective vision in reaching the goths and those on the fringe of the youth population of Chichester. The same can happen in your church with your people groups.

6. Detached youth work

This is really taking seriously the mandate of Jesus in

Matthew 28:16–20 'to go', although the detached of the title refers to the youth, rather than the youth workers! The work should always be done from and to a church base, with the youth workers working in pairs, preferably male and female, so as to be able to approach either sex on the streets. It can be done based around questionnaires, but is best done working in a very informal way into the youth of a town, operating according to their numbers and meeting places. Often it will be found that this is long-term work in the sense of building up relationships, trust, the permission to pray for and eventually with young people, and the eventual extension of invitations to special youth events. Often when commitments are made, the discipleship process will have to be at least initially restricted to the same sort of approach, ie, discipleship with 'ad hoc' bible studies being done on the streets, and then eventually with small groups of twos and threes in the homes of the youth workers.

Initial apparent success with detached youth work is very limited, or can be spectacular and then spectacularly hard to follow through! It is, none-the-less, both biblical and very worth while as a seed-sowing exercise, and in the long-term can garner fruit where originally there would have been no possibility of the fruit of the gospel growing in the lives of the individuals. Detached youth work is the only way some youth will hear.

7. Summer schemes

These have already been hinted at above. It may be appropriate in your town, village or city to organise a particular summer scheme to cater for young people during their break from school. It may equally be necessary to cater for them during the time that they initially leave school and head towards short- or long-term unemployment. Thus training on life-related skills, job interviews, producing curriculum vitae, and so on, may all be helpful. Similarly helpful might be sports-related projects, where for example a week of training and teaching the rudiments of American football culminates in a game together at the end of that week, and a final Saturday evening barbecue, for example. Identifying effectively a specific geographical area (helpful not only for goal setting, but also to avoid any possibility of territorial argument amongst young people) can be done with an erected marquee serving as a base for the week for refreshments, music, videos, discussions, preaching and meetings. It does need to be said that in working with unchurched youth in this way, such summer schemes need to be repeated at least three or four years in a row before fruit is seen. It would be a mistake to call a halt to such a project on the basis of 'failure' if no fruit is seen after the first one or two years.

8. Church meetings

While it is true that all of our church meetings need to be 'seeker sensitive' in that they are relevant and accessible to the average enquiring non-Christian, some of them should be specifically 'seeker targeted', and I would plead that this needs to be the case for youth as much as for anyone else. A seeker targeted young person's meeting should not be too remote from the life of the normal church so that there is a massive credibility gap when a new convert seeks to make the transition into the life of the church. This in itself is a challenge to a 'normal' church meeting. I would suggest that such a meeting needs to be short, lively, well-explained, fast moving, varied, and should incorporate culturally acceptable music (this will need careful evaluation as an area where rave music is popular may be different to one where house music is the norm, or heavy metal, and again for soul music). Audio-visuals, lighting, public address systems, short interviews, *short* talks (helped by visual aids and stories), opportunity for small group discussion and feedback, being pro-active rather than static, and involving people in moving around from item to item, using creative visual backdrops, using drama (where it is good and not merely twee), and having opportunities for response and ministry – all of these are youth seeker sensitive issues. Think them through one by one.

9. Church youth group meetings

All of the above applies to these, though the choice of topic under discussion might be more specifically related to youth (eg, peer group pressure, self-identity, sex and sexuality, war and peace and green issues).

10. Uniformed organisations

These have traditionally been both a strength and weakness of the denominational churches. Many such churches now seeking to be evangelistic in their emphasis find themselves inheriting a very nebulously church-connected organisation, whose main function seems to be social. It is not easy, though not impossible, to turn such an orientation around, and ways of doing this need to be found which are more creative than merely insisting that the scouts attend the family parade service once a month! The deliberate prayer strategy that prays new, Holy Spirit-filled leaders in to positions of influence, and which prays for the club's members as well, is a part of this process. So too is the setting up of regular, relevant, Christian orientated visiting speakers, musicians, dramatists, escapologists, DJs, and so on. Organised trips away on adventure weekends, houseparties and the like, are a part of the same process. The principle is one of finding ways to take church to the group, rather than to try to get the group to come to the church. Thus putting together resource packages for the group which are clearly

Christian in orientation, but relevant, radical and professional in their approach, will be much appreciated not only by your average cub or scout group, but also by its Christian/non-Christian leaders! Such creative packages can include: drama workshops, video-making workshops, make-up workshops, film showings, organised concerts and visits to seeker targeted guest meetings.

Finally, given that we have noted that the optimum age for conversion in western society is fourteen years and nine months, and also given that the most effective evangelists and witnesses are usually those who are most recently converted (because of their zealousness and also because of their network of non-Christian friends), and given that evangelism in a homogenous unit (peer group) is the most successful anyway, it *must* be a sound investment to identify, motivate, teach, and train our committed Christian youth to best evangelise their own peers. Such motivation, teaching and training (in that specific order) will need to be creative, pro-active and culturally relevant, as well as being practical in its orientation. I would suggest that it needs to cover as a minimum the following topics:

Who – The concept that while only ten per cent of the young people you are addressing are likely to be Spirit of Jesus-anointed evangelists (Eph 4:11–13), none the less *everyone* is called to be a witness for Christ.

Whom – Relevant teaching and inspiration on God's heart for young people and the concept of friendship evangelism, with practical teaching on identifying networks, naming individuals, developing friendships, exposure to and not imposure of their Christian faith, and the principle of including non-Christians in friendship and conversations, until they exclude themselves.

Why – The biblical and our personal motivations for evangelism.

Why not – The personal factors which stop us becoming

involved in evangelism, eg, fear, embarrassment, apathy, wrong teaching and sin.

What – The nature of the gospel which we share, including practical teaching on incarnational communication – being and not having good news – the gospel in words, works and wonders, which is Christocentric.

Whose territory – Some practical teaching on the nature of spiritual warfare, praise and worship, and prayer, as they relate to evangelism.

Whose responsibility – A session aimed at reducing pressure on adolescents in evangelism, to demonstrate God's desire and ability to see people saved and our inability to do likewise.

How – Several sessions on personal witnessing, covering; booking God appointments, putting ourselves under obligation to other people, stimulating interest, starting conversations and provoking a reaction, using the Holy Spirit's power in evangelism for fruit in our own lives, conviction of sin, and spiritual gifts. Also dealing with 'red herrings', including the principle of re-focusing difficult questions. Plus basic principles of communication.

Conversion – How to actually lead someone through to Christ.

Using your story – Teaching on the use of personal testimony.

I have sought to deal with all of these subjects in three chapters (one in my *The Teenage Survival Kit*, and two in its follow-up, *The Teenage Revival Kit*, both published by Kingsway), albeit in a limited medium, ie, the printed page. I recommend that since such material was written for young people, you might wish to have a look at it before in turn recommending it to the young people for whom you are responsible.

Obviously, trained, equipped and committed young Christians need to be represented by a good percentage ratio in the life of any church's evangelism team, which in itself needs to constitute between ten to fifteen per cent of the church membership list. It would be my overall recommendation as a working evangelist that fifty per cent of any church's budget (by which I mean not only finances but also allocation of resources such as personnel and premises) goes on maintenance, and fifty per cent on extension, ie, evangelism. Of the fifty per cent which goes on evangelism, I would recommend that fifty per cent of that is itself directed towards young people and youth outreach and discipling, ie, twenty-five per cent of the church's total budget.

And so we come to the end of what I hope has been a helpful exploration of the mind, heart, and world of the average adolescent, given of course that there is no such thing as an average adolescent! I have sought in this book to intertwine the theoretical with the practical, basing it as I have not only on research, but on personal experience over the course of the last fourteen years. As I promised at the outset of the book, this has not been a manual on parenting – as I close this book our daughter, Frederica Clare (our first child) is just over twelve months old, and we have much to learn in that realm! Rather, it is an honest attempt to make sense of my experience and hopefully yours, and to provide along the way a few pointers which will better help us to understand the complex world of the adolescent. It has consistently been my experience that whenever I have taught on this subject, the seminars and workshops which I have held have been at least fifty per cent attended by adolescents themselves, many of whom have subsequently expressed some gratitude for the light which God was able to shed on their development.

So it might be that at the end of the day this book is written not only for all of you delighted and frustrated parents, youth leaders, teachers and youth evangelists, but also for those incredibly complex and infinitely rewarding young lives that God has entrusted you with, and to whom God has given *you* as at least part of his answer. So, if the book has been of any help to you at all, perhaps the best advice would be: pass it on to an adolescent!

SOURCES OF SCHOOLWORK MATERIALS

British Youth for Christ
Cleobury Place
Cleobury Mortimer
Nr Kidderminster
Worcs
DY14 8JG

Tel: (0299) 270260

Scripture Union
130 City Road
London
EC1V 2NJ

Tel: 071-250 1966

Interschools Christian Fellowship
(Address and telephone as above)

THE DILEMMA OF SELF-ESTEEM

Alister and Joanna McGrath

Low self-esteem can be a crippler. It can hinder people from achieving their potential. It can sabotage relationships and careers. It can keep even the most dedicated Christians from fulfilling God's purpose for their lives.

Yet so many who promote positive self-esteem have ignored the reality of sin and the need for humility. Often the price paid for positive self-esteem is a dilution of the gospel. So how should Christians deal with the problem of a negative self-image?

The path to the answer leads through some intriguing terrain. Human infants in all cultures follow a basic, primal instinct to attach emotionally to parents (or another close adult). Given a choice, infants often prefer love to food. Even higher forms of animal life exhibit attachment behaviour. But a separation of mother and infant (perceived by the child as abandonment) may disturb this attachment, damaging the child's self-esteem. So for the Christian, once separated from God by sin, self-worth and acceptance are grounded in an attachment to God through Christ.

In this important book, the McGraths take the best of recent psychological research and set it alongside a responsible Biblical approach to the subject. They point out the valid insights of modern psychology,, but at the same time, they deal with the tensions between the gospel and most secular psychotherapies. Here is an in-depth, sensitive analysis of a crucial subject for the church.

Joanna McGrath is principal clinical psychologist at the Rivermead Rehabilitation Unit in Oxford, England.

Alister McGrath, author of many books and frequent conference speaker, teaches theology at Wycliffe Hall, Oxford University.

HEALING LIFE'S HIDDEN ADDICTIONS
Dr. Archibald Hart

Self-Hatred ● *Worry* ● *Entertainment* ● *Food* ● *Sex* ● *Shopping*
Work ● *Codependency* ● *Control* ● *Exercise*

So, you don't take drugs, you don't have a drink problem, you gave up smoking years ago. So, you don't have to worry about addictions?

In *Healing Life's Hidden Addictions*, Dr Hart explores fascinating new research which shows that our inner compulsions are addictive, and not only do they waste much of our time, but they also control our lives.

In addition to offering sound medical and psychological insight, Hart probes deeply into the spiritual dynamics of addiction and points the way for release from them.

'I think it is quite brilliant. I found the book professional, very interesting, informative, thorough, with clear definitions and helpful conclusions. There is a good balance between the physical, psychological and spiritual.'

Helena Wilkinson, author and lecturer for CWR, and editor of
The Christian Counsellor

Dr Archibald Hart is a prolific author and Dean in a school of psychology researching the most effective ways of overcoming addictive behaviours.

A PASSION FOR HOLINESS

J. I. Packer

Changing our lives for the better

The sequel to *Keep in Step with the Spirit*.

'This will take our best thinking and our most faithful living.'

Richard Foster

'No one is better qualified to address this call.'

Chuck Colson

As Christians succumb more and more to materialism, holiness is becoming the forgotten virtue of the Church. Yet, as the Bible makes clear, holiness is high on God's priorities for his people.

J. I. Packer brings us back to where God wants us to be. He shows us that holiness is nothing less than a lifelong passion for loving God and following his ways.

J. I. Packer is Professor of Systematic and Historical Theology at Regent College, Vancouver, Canada, and has also held posts in his native Britain. Dr. Packer is the author of numerous best-sellers including *Knowing God*, *Keep in Step with the Spirit* and most recently *Among God's Giants*.

PROPHET
A NOVEL
Frank E. Peretti

' You will know the truth, and the truth will set you free' (John 8: 32)

John Barrett, anchorman for 'NewsSix at Five', the city's most watched newscast, has a problem. His comfortable, successful world is being jarred to breaking point. He's caught his producer skewing a story to fit her own prejudices, then lying to cover her tracks – and she appears to be hiding something much bigger. His father's 'accidental' death suddenly isn't looking so accidental. Carl, his estranged son, has returned to challenge his integrity and probe to find the man behind the TV image. The supposedly professional and objective newsroom is now divided and fighting over Truth. And what are these mysterious 'voices' Barrett is hearing ...?

Once again, master storyteller **Frank Peretti** has woven a prophetic tale for our times. *Prophet* carries all the hallmarks of Frank's blockbusting fiction – plenty of edge-of-the-seat action, nail-biting suspense, breakneck pacing, and blow-you-out-of-the-water spiritual impact. But more than this, it penetrates to the very heart of a vast struggle that threatens to tear our society to pieces, the struggle over which vision of moral authority will define our nation.